Animals that Show & Tell

Animals that Show & Tell

William L. Coleman

BETHANY HOUSE PUBLISHERS
MINNEAPOLIS, MINNESOTA 55438
A Division of Bethany Fellowship, Inc.

Illustrations by Chris Wold Dyrud

Published by Bethany House Publishers
A Division of Bethany Fellowship, Inc.
6820 Auto Club Road, Minneapolis, Minnesota 55438

Printed in the United States of America

Library of Congress Cataloging in Publication Data

Coleman, William L.
    Animals that show and tell.

    Summary: Descriptions of the roadrunner, python, black widow spider, and other wonders of nature demonstrate spiritual truth and the validity of living according to Christian faith. Biblical quotations follow each passage.
    1. Children—Prayer-books and devotions—English. 2. Animals—Religious aspects—Christianity—Juvenile literature. [1. Animals—Miscellanea. 2. Prayer books and devotions. 3. Christian life] I. Title.
BV4870.C62   1985   242'.62   85-15122
ISBN 0-87123-807-1 (pbk.)

WILLIAM L. COLEMAN is a graduate of the Washington Bible College in Washington, D.C., and Grace Theological Seminary in Winona Lake, Indiana.

He has pastored three churches: a Baptist church in Michigan, a Mennonite church in Kansas, and an Evangelical Free Church in Aurora, Nebraska. He is a Staley Foundation lecturer.

The author of 75 magazine articles, his by-line has appeared in *Christianity Today, Eternity, Good News Broadcaster, Campus Life, Moody Monthly, Evangelical Beacon,* and *The Christian Reader.* Besides the children's devotional series, Coleman is also the author of the Chesapeake Charlie series, mysteries for ages 10–14.

Other Books in the Coleman Family Devotional Series

Listen to the Animals
Singing Penguins and Puffed-Up Toads
Counting Stars
Good Night Book
Sleep Tight Book
My Magnificent Machine
More About My Magnificent Machine
On Your Mark
Today I Feel Like a Warm Fuzzy
Today I Feel Loved
Today I Feel Shy

Other Books on Special Family Topics by Coleman

Getting Ready for Our New Baby
Making TV Work for Your Family
Getting Ready for My First Day of School
My Hospital Book

Contents

11 • Acorns for Dinner
14 • House Hunting
16 • Walking on Water
18 • Playing in the Snow
20 • The Bad-Luck Bird
22 • What Good Are Mushrooms?
25 • Turtles Are Tanks
27 • What Guides the Butterfly?
29 • The Missing Python
32 • What Good Is a Dead Tree?
35 • Look at the Facts
37 • Getting Away
39 • Fathers Make a Difference
42 • Ants Keep Livestock
45 • Why Finches Don't Freeze
47 • How Much Wood Does a Woodchuck Chuck?
50 • Even Lions Get the Blues
52 • Squirrels Are Acrobats
55 • Sheep Living in the Mountains
57 • Monkeys with Large Noses
59 • When Elephants Get Thirsty
61 • Fur Coat for Your House
63 • Marmots Like to Play
65 • The Arctic Fox
68 • The Mighty Amazon
70 • How Smart Are You?
73 • The Skunk Pig
75 • Swinging Monkeys
77 • How Good Is Your Memory?
79 • Cleaning Animals
82 • Dogs Are Friends
84 • The Moose Is Back
86 • Wild Horses
89 • Do Roadrunners Go "Beep Beep"?
92 • It's Cooler at the Beach
94 • Avoid This Animal
96 • Do Spiders Have Ears?

98 • The Brave Pigeon
100 • Some Snakes Are Wimps
102 • Counting Fish Scales
104 • When the Sting Is Gone
106 • Not Looking for Trouble
108 • The Mantis Parent
110 • Building Stone Houses
112 • The Young Deer
114 • Stuck Up a Tree
116 • Who Loves Mosquitoes?
118 • The Wirey Weasel
121 • Can Quicksand Swallow You?
123 • The Intelligent Raven
125 • Black Widow Spiders at Work
127 • Chimps Are Comedians

Look What God Created

Today you can imagine yourself racing across the desert with a funny little roadrunner. Maybe you would rather learn about the pigeon who was a war hero. How would you like to meet a 30-foot snake along the Amazon River, or watch a raven steal your keys, or run with wild horses in the West?

God made a world filled with all of these fabulous creatures. You can meet many of them in the pages of this volume. As you read about them, you might also better understand a God who cares about you—every day.

William L. Coleman
Aurora, Nebraska

one

Acorns for Dinner

Can you picture a bowl of toasted acorns sitting on your table? How about opening your lunch bag at school and pulling out a handful of tasty acorns? Maybe you could walk up to the counter in a fast-food restaurant and ask for a hamburger and an order of acorns.

People used to eat a great many acorns, and some scientists believe we still should. Some Europeans eat them. If you choose to eat acorns, the chestnut oak would probably be best. They are the largest acorns, reaching two inches in size. Roasting helps bring out the sweet flavor.

A wide variety of animals and birds depend on acorns for their diets. Insects drill holes in them and deposit eggs so their larvae will have food when they hatch.

One of the most active acorn eaters is the acorn woodpecker. This hard worker drills holes in old fence posts and carefully stuffs an acorn into each space. He has his own vending machine. The woodpecker will simply return and withdraw one as he needs it; that is, if they are still there. Squirrels enjoy stealing these acorns if they can find the right fence post.

There seems to be no honor among the animals who eat acorns. Instead of taking enough time to gather their own, they spend much of their time stealing from each other. Squirrels cart the acorns off from woodpeckers. Bears steal them from squirrels.

Some acorn collectors such as the woodpecker go to great lengths to hide their food, but others like the red squirrel merely

place them in heaps on the ground. Naturally they get ripped off quite often.

All acorns come from oak trees and there are 58 different types of oak trees in the United States.

Oregon and California grow beautiful acorns. The Canyon Live Oak produces an acorn with a bright golden fuzz. At first you might think you've discovered something valuable, and of course you have found a beautiful part of nature.

When the acorn crop is plentiful, nature seems to prosper. Deer are more plentiful, bears have more cubs and animals like coyotes have additional small game to eat.

Some animals eat acorns whenever it is convenient. Others store them for winter. The fox squirrel tries to prepare itself for the sudden, cold change in nature. It takes time to bury acorns, hoping to have enough to last through the tough winter season. Fox squirrels know they need to store up for tomorrow.

Smart people do the same thing. They are interested in more than just today. While they live on earth, they like to do some things that are important forever. That is why Christians feed the hungry. It's the reason they clothe children and help educate the poor. They know they are doing good things that will be valuable to God—forever.

"Tell them to use their money to do good. They should be rich in good works and should give happily to those in need, always being ready to share with others whatever God has given them. By doing this they will be storing up real treasure for themselves in heaven—it is the only safe investment for eternity!" (1 Tim. 6:18, 19).

1. How does a woodpecker store acorns?
2. How many different types of acorns are there in the United States?
3. What are some things Christians can do that are important forever?

two

House Hunting

Almost all creatures need a good place to live. They need a dry place to hide from the rain or a high place to keep them safe from enemies. That is why most animals and birds spend much of their time building homes and nests. They want to protect themselves and their newborn children.

The wren is one of the busiest birds when it comes to preparing a home. It is the father wren's job to prepare a good place to live. Usually the mother bird refuses to have anything to do with him until he has a place ready.

In the early spring the father wren goes to work looking for housing. He is searching for something already made. He would like to redecorate it himself. House hunting takes him to rusty tin cans, abandoned birdhouses and even nests.

Once he discovers the right dwelling, he begins to furnish it to match his taste. Twigs, sticks, string and other materials are added until it looks comfortable.

However, the wren knows that his work is not finished. He must find a couple more houses and decorate them, too. The female wren will want to inspect several of his houses before she makes her final decision.

When his job is complete, the wren starts singing in hopes the female will come to his "Open House." If she agrees to live in one of the houses, she will then select some feathers of her own choosing and rearrange the nest. Only then will she agree to lay her eggs.

This is far from being the end of the father's work. He must now serve as the protector of the eggs. After they hatch he joins mother in the endless search for food for the chicks. They comb the area for every insect they can find. For a solid month they will continue their search. Each will gather over a hundred pieces of food.

After the chicks are old enough to feed themselves, the father wren starts all over again. He begins to redecorate in hopes of beginning another set of chicks that same summer.

Just as birds need places to live, so do human beings. We not only need a home in this world, but we also want a home in heaven. Jesus told us that there are many places to live with our Heavenly Father. He promised to go to heaven and prepare a place for us to live forever. We don't know what "homes" will be like in heaven, but we believe that our Father has some great places for us.

By believing in Jesus Christ you and I reserve a place in heaven. God the Father will take care of everything for us.

"There are many homes up there where my Father lives, and I am going to prepare them for your coming. When everything is ready, then I will come and get you" (John 14:2).

1. How does a wren prepare a house?
2. What does a male wren do after he has prepared the nests?
3. What do you think your home in heaven will be like?

15

three

Walking on Water

If you saw an animal walking on water, you would have to look twice. You would rub your eyes, stare and step closer to get a better look. Everyone knows that something cannot walk on water. And yet, something does.

We are talking about the small water shrew, a six-inch-long creature that lives around shallow pools. Half its size is tail, but the busy shrew eats all the time. That's why it keeps on the move in constant search of food. At least that is one reason. It also keeps moving because trout and other fish would like to eat this speedy animal.

When the water shrew has its choice, it likes to dine on water spiders and a few small fish. However, usually it will eat almost anything that gets in its path.

Since most of its time is spent around the water, this shrew has learned how to use the water. The water shrew can dive or merely take a casual float across the pond. But its most amazing feat is walking on top of the water.

It doesn't merely look like the water shrew is walking on water. And it isn't fooling everyone by tiptoeing across the rocks. Its feet are made in such a special way that it can stay on top.

The bottoms of the water shrew's feet are covered with tiny hairs. Small air bubbles become trapped in these hairs as if there were small balloons on the soles of its feet.

When a shrew races across the water, it is traveling at a high speed. Its speed plus the balloons under its feet allow the shrew to stay on top of the water.

Since a water shrew can shoot quickly over the top of the water, it can surprise most of its victims and grab them before they know what is coming.

Walking on water is almost impossible, but the small water shrew is an exciting exception. Ships are also exceptions because of the way they are built. It is especially unusual when we hear of a human who can walk on top of water without anything to help him. Jesus Christ was able to walk on water, not because He had balloons under His feet or because He knew where the rocks were. Jesus could walk on water because God helped Him. He had the power to make waves calm down, make children walk, and cause the blind to see. Many people followed Jesus because they believed He had a special power from God and yet He was still kind, loving and forgiving.

"He saw that they were in serious trouble, rowing hard and struggling against the wind and waves. About three o'clock in the morning he walked out to them on the water" (Mark 6:48).

1. Name an amazing thing about the water shrew.
2. What does the water shrew eat?
3. Name an amazing thing that Jesus Christ has done.

four

Playing in the Snow

Parents might groan a little when they see snow beginning to fall. But there are so many good uses for the white fluff that snow must be one of God's best gifts.

Eskimos learn to accept snow as a friend. Instead of slowing down their lives, it actually speeds things up. They use snow as a highway. With their dogsleds and snowmobiles, they can get around much faster if the ground is covered with snow.

It also works to protect their homes from the terrible cold of the north. If snow is packed against a house, it helps keep the cold air out and it also locks the warm air in. Snow holds air between its flakes and refuses to allow colder air to push past it.

Snow provides an excellent playground for people of all ages as well as for animals. Without snow we couldn't make snowballs, build snowmen, ride sleds or go skiing. While you and I are playing on top of the snow, some of nature's animals are traveling beneath it. Beavers spend their winters under the snow-covered ice, coming up for short trips. The holes they leave lead to their snug living quarters.

Some tiny rodents live under the snow and try to avoid coming up too often. Foxes, owls and hawks wait for any small animal to poke its head above the snow. Without the snow cover, many of these little creatures would be captured easily by their enemies.

Snow is an excellent source of water in many parts of the north. If it melts slowly, the earth receives moisture to help the vegetation in the spring. However, if too much snow melts quickly, some areas begin to flood.

The beautiful snowflake takes on a great change after it settles on the ground. Often six-sided, flakes are shaped in a great many ways. But after they hit the ground, the flakes become granular. The heat of the earth plus evaporation cause them to shrink and change form.

Snow has an extra benefit that we sometimes forget. It often makes people stop and think. Snow closes roads, cancels schools, makes airplanes stay on the ground. It causes families to spend the evening together drinking hot chocolate and getting to know each other better. We have to stop hurrying around and think about what is really important in life. It gives us a chance to think about the majesty of God and spend time with the people we love.

"For he directs the snow, the showers, and storm to fall upon the earth. Man's work stops at such a time, so that all men everywhere may recognize his power" (Job 37:6, 7).

1. How does snow help the Eskimos?
2. Think of an animal and the way snow helps it.
3. What do you like best about snow?

five

The Bad-Luck Bird

Hundreds of years ago the magpie got a bad reputation and this reputation has hung on. Stories are easy to start but they are tough to get rid of.

The story of the magpie bird probably got started because of its neatness and attractiveness. In some forgotten conversation an individual suggested that the magpie was a close friend of Satan and probably worked for him.

Once the rumor started, it was easy to prove. Someone said that every Friday magpies left for a secret meeting with the devil. People looked around on Fridays and guess what? It did seem hard to find a magpie just before the weekend. Maybe there was some truth to this story.

And had anyone noticed the magpie's tongue? Didn't it look *extra* red. It sort of looked like it was dripping blood.

With evidence like this and the willingness to believe anything, some people kept these stories going. They told these tales to their children who in turn told them to their children.

The superstitious stories jumped the Atlantic Ocean and when early Americans saw magpies they became afraid. They believed the magpie could bring them bad luck since it worked for Satan. If farmers saw magpies in their fields, some thought their crops would fail. And naturally a few crops did fail. When mothers saw magpies flying near their homes, some were frightened that one of their children might die. And naturally a few children did die.

As you might imagine, few people wanted magpies around.

If someone saw one, he might shoot it, throw stones at it or even try to cast a net over it. They were going to kill the "Devil Bird" and all its relatives.

Today the white magpie, the black magpie and their relatives live fairly normal bird lives. They face all the natural dangers other birds encounter, but the deep superstition no longer follows them.

Often we say things that are bad and we don't really know the facts. Hurting the reputation of a bird is bad enough, but frequently we injure the lives of people by unkind words.

As Chrisitans we ought to guard our tongues. It's a shame to injure human beings simply because we enjoy saying evil things.

"A good man thinks before he speaks; the evil man pours out his evil words without a thought" (Prov. 15:28).

1. What are some stories that were told about magpies?
2. What was the nickname of the magpie?
3. Have you known someone who was hurt by what someone else said about him?

six

What Good Are Mushrooms?

Mushrooms can taste good and they can have beautiful colors, but what is their real job in the woods? Probably their most important role is to attach themselves to dead logs and slowly take them apart. If it were not for the mushrooms, the forest would be stacked with old wood.

A mushroom does not have seeds because it is not a plant.

A mushroom is a fungus and therefore gives off spores. Sometimes the spores are seen in patches like snow, but an individual spore is too small to be seen without a microscope.

Spores have an amazing ability to get around. Some have been found as high as 35,000 feet up. That is as high as the large commercial planes fly.

When a spore finds a place to attach to, it soon begins to grow. Mushrooms do not need light so they are often tucked away in dark corners or under leaves. Some will build slowly as strands come together. Others, like shaggy ink cap mushrooms, seem to jump up overnight.

Called "saprophytes," mushrooms must take their valuable food from the dying forest. They have no green leaves to help them. By reaching into dead wood they pull out important food sources. Robbed of its strength, the dead log will begin to decay and fall apart.

Mushroom hunting has become a popular sport. People enjoy eating them on pizzas and other good foods. However, mushrooms can also be very dangerous if you eat the wrong kinds.

Children should be discouraged from picking mushrooms and eating them by themselves. Even if you think you can tell eatable from noneatable mushrooms, it is still easy to be fooled.

It would be better if no child ever ate mushrooms from the

DYRUD

field unless he first checked with his parents. The wrong mushrooms can make you terribly sick. Parents can usually make good judgments or tell you how to find out.

In many ways that is exactly why the Bible is like our parents. It gives us warnings so we can avoid trouble. Without some direction, it's easy to make terrible mistakes. The Bible has wisdom, direction and love. As the Word of God, the Bible leads us so we can get the best out of life.

"I am not writing about these things to make you ashamed, but to warn and counsel you as beloved children" (1 Cor. 4:14).

1. What is the most important role of mushrooms?
2. Do mushrooms need light to grow?
3. How is the Bible a guide for you?

seven

Turtles Are Tanks

Our friends, Mona and Kim, have a turtle as a pet. Actually it was given to their mother years ago and she has taken good care of it. The children have grown up with the turtle and it's practically a member of their family. Turtles are one of the more popular pets among children.

In order to discuss turtles, we should begin by learning two words. The "carapace" is the camper or top shell, which comes in a variety of colors and shapes. Its color helps the turtle to hide in a bush or in water. This shell is connected to the turtle's body and the turtle cannot step out of it.

The second word is "plastron." This is the bottom plate of bone that covers the turtle's chest. It, too, is part of its body.

If you see a box turtle hiding in the forest, look for its trapdoor. When the box turtle pulls itself into its shell, a door closes to cover its head for protection. It sticks its head out of the door to feast on beetles, spiders and other choice delights.

When you get a chance to taste cooked turtle, you should certainly try some. With its good flavor, turtle is a popular food in some areas of the country.

One of the main reasons why turtles continue to survive in a crowded, polluted world is their ability to change eating habits. When man has ruined certain rivers and killed their shellfish, the map turtle simply switches diets and eats insects and dead fish.

Most turtles we see range from a few inches in length up to a foot long. However, a few rare turtles become massive. The famous Giant Tortoise reaches an amazing four feet in length and weighs in at nearly 500 pounds. Because of accurate records we know that members of this species have lived for more than 100 years.

Another large variety is the seagoing loggerhead turtle. More a submarine than a tank, it supports its 500 pound body by eating such delicacies as the man-of-war, which looks a lot like a jellyfish.

Among the more famous turtles is the snapping turtle. While most turtles cannot hurt you, this one could make a nasty wound. Found on both land and water, its snap is quick and strong.

The majority of turtles look mean but they avoid most fights. Usually a turtle will merely draw its head and legs inside its shell and wait for the attacker to go away. An animal might yell at the turtle and jump on it, but the rock-like creature just sits tight.

If a turtle tried to fight, it would leave itself open to get hurt. Should it try to run away, the turtle would be easily caught.

Consequently, it merely takes its stand and sits tight. It refuses to be moved. When the enemy is done ranting and raving, it will get disgusted and leave. But not the turtle. The green tank keeps its cool and stands its ground. It wins almost every time.

Sometimes Christians would do well to imitate turtles. They don't need to back down and they don't need to run. Christians can draw a line and say, "I won't do that," or "I must do this." They don't need to fight and they don't need to run. They can do what they know is right no matter what other people do.

"Put on all of God's armor so that you will be able to stand safe against all strategies and tricks of Satan" (Eph. 6:11).

1. Tell about a turtle's top shell.
2. Tell about a box turtle's trapdoor.
3. Tell how you have stood your ground as a Christian.

eight

What Guides the Butterfly?

Usually we think of butterflies as weak little creatures that float around flowers. If we understood them better, we would realize how tough they really are.

One big surprise may be to discover that they are fighters. If another butterfly drifts into their territory, a bruising battle may break out. The war can become so violent that their wings can be torn and the butterfly left unable to take to the air.

These large winged beauties cannot afford to sit around and enjoy nature. Nectar is their food and they must move constantly to find enough. This hunt serves nature well as the butterfly also picks up pollen and transfers it from plant to plant.

A painted lady butterfly will light gently on a flower and put its long tube tongue to work. Drinking up the nectar, the butterfly brushes against the pinhead size pollen. Pollen must be transported to another plant within a couple of hours and put in place. Drifting off to the next flower, the butterfly leaves the pollen with the ovule. This union allows seeds to form.

Sometimes their work of cross-pollination takes butterflies to unusual places. In the summer the meadows near the Arctic Circle also need to swap pollen. When their time arrives, butterflies will carry out the job.

One of nature's most beautiful butterflies, the monarch, makes it a point to stay away from cold areas. If freezing weather hits the monarch, it can't possibly survive. That's why they keep moving south as cool temperatures start chasing them.

They believe Canada is a good place to visit but they wouldn't want to live there.

Their trips south have been traced and their winter resort area discovered. Monarchs are aiming for sunny Mexico. Once there they will set up quarters in the mountains. Millions of monarchs live in the trees and wait to head back north. Some of their friends lounge around Florida and California.

Scientists do not yet fully understand how a simple butterfly can find its way to Mexico and back to Canada. The insect does not seem capable of calculating the trip. Nevertheless, God has put some sort of guidance system in this fragile creature. It is an inner guidance system that does a great job from year to year.

People also need guidance. They need to recognize good and evil so they can choose between the two. If we are Christians, God lives inside us to be our guide. He helps us pick and choose when decisions become really hard.

"For this great God is our God forever and ever. He will be our guide until we die" (Ps. 48:14).

1. What is the food of butterflies?
2. Where do monarchs spend the winter?
3. How do you know when God is guiding you?

nine

The Missing Python

How hard would it be to lose a nine-foot-long python snake? That is exactly what happened in a town in Nebraska, and as you might guess the neighbors were a little concerned. Especially since this was the second python to escape in that same area.

The owner of the python tried to get everyone to remain calm by assuring them that his long friend wasn't very dangerous. He insisted that it was not strong enough to crush an adult and barely had the bite of a cat.

But where could a nine foot python hide? Practically anywhere it wants to. Because of its color and ability to slide into small places, pythons are difficult to see unless they choose to come out. The snake was found beneath a tree in a local backyard.

Pythons are one of the most amazing and mysterious snakes. They are not, however, completely harmless. A child in Iowa was reportedly killed by just such a creature. Despite the friendly nature of some animals, many can become dangerous at the most unexpected times.

Snakes continue to hold our attention for several reasons. One reason is that many stories have been told about snakes that are fascinating but not necessarily true. A second reason is that sometimes we imagine that snake eyes have a strange power. A third reason is that we seem to believe that most snakes are extremely deadly and must be killed on sight.

Naturally we should stay away from any snake if we don't

know what kind it is. However, most snakes are harmless. The problem often is that we don't know enough about them to be able to tell the good ones from the bad ones.

If you want to study snakes, a python would be as interesting as any. Pythons are long and like to climb trees. They are not poisonous but have a tight grip and can crush small animals. Many of its prey are small enough to swallow in one gulp.

A python can be a beautiful creature. The longest reach thirty feet. That would make ten of your longest steps. Sometime step off ten *long* strides in front of your house and try to imagine how long some of these reptiles are.

Those who study snakes have found a few surprises with the python. There are tiny legs along its body. These legs consist of a small bone covered with some type of skin.

Why does a python need legs? They do not use them to walk but rather crawl like other snakes. Scientists believe that the boa is the only other snake with legs. Studies continue in hope that science will find out if they have a purpose.

Presently we have many fears about snakes. Some of our fears are based on facts but most are myths. God has promised us a day when all creatures will live in perfect peace. We will have nothing to fear from snakes and they will have nothing to fear from us. It will be a good time of harmony in the world.

"Babies will crawl safely among poisonous snakes, and a little child who puts his hand in a nest of deadly adders will pull it out unharmed" (Isa. 11:8).

1. Are the majority of snakes harmless or harmful?
2. How long are pythons?
3. Describe the time, as you picture it will be, when nature will be in harmony.

ten

What Good Is a Dead Tree?

Have you ever looked at a small log and thought how dead and still it was? But if you picked it up you found a number of bugs and insects crawling around on the ground. It looked lifeless, but underneath a tiny world bustled about.

The same thing may be true of the dead tree you drive past on the way to school each day. All of its leaves are gone, but that doesn't mean there is no life there. Both inside and out there could be a wide variety of living creatures.

If a tree is dead and still standing, scientists call it a snag. You might want to leave a snag standing on your property because of all the good it is able to do. In fact, some animals would far rather have a big snag around than a tall healthy tree.

The eruption of Mt. St. Helens left thousands of snag trees. Soon afterwards creatures began to inhabit those trees and are flourishing today.

The loose bark of a snag makes it an excellent home for many insects. A number of beetles like to snuggle under the bark and lay their eggs. Ants also find the soft wood easy living quarters for their young.

Since insects enjoy living in a dead tree, birds will also find it attractive. Some birds, like the woodpecker, stick around searching for meals in the soft wood. Other birds enjoy snags because of their height. Hawks use them as towers so they can scan the nearby territory. When a hawk spots a mouse, it strikes quickly and picks it up as food.

By removing all dead trees we also chase away many of the

DYRUD

valuable insect eating birds. If we leave some snags, we furnish them with dependable feeding grounds. The birds return the favor by cleaning up other insects in your area.

Birds such as owls, chickadees, nuthatches, wrens and woodpeckers may want to live near your house. An inviting dead tree could make that possible.

When squirrels can find a suitable hole in a snag, they may move in and store their food for the winter. Raccoons will look it over, too, for a neat den. Before long this "dead" tree can become a sizeable apartment house.

If conditions are correct, a dead log could turn into stone. This is called becoming petrified. Slowly each particle in the wood is replaced by other particles. Most of these particles are supplied by water washing lime into the log. As stone washes in and wood washes out, the log still holds its original form. Eventually it ends up as a stone log, but this takes many, many years.

Nature has many ways of taking things that are dead and using them for life again. Vegetation becomes food for other plants. Dead trees fall to the ground and after long periods of time become coal. Seeds go under the soil, die and become beautiful plants.

People die too. If they believe in Jesus Christ, they stay alive in heaven. A person who places his or her faith in Christ will live forever with God and His Son.

Death becomes life. It happens often in the woods and fields. It also happens among people. Those who die, trusting in Jesus Christ, continue to live—forever.

"Jesus told her, 'I am the one who raises the dead and gives them life again. Anyone who believes in me, even though he dies like anyone else, shall live again'" (John 11:25).

1. What is a snag?
2. How does a dead tree provide homes for insects and animals?
3. What do you think this means: "When we die and leave these bodies—we will have wonderful new bodies in heaven, homes that will be ours forevermore, made for us by God himself, and not by human hands" (2 Cor. 5:1)?

eleven

Look at the Facts

Hummingbirds do not hum. They move their wings so fast that a humming sound is made. Those swift little wings race at 4,000 times each minute.

A baby sea otter can float long before it can swim. The air trapped in its fur helps hold the otter up.

A walrus has 400 whiskers that help it feel the bottom of the sea when it searches for food. Because of restrictions on walrus hunting, their numbers have tripled in recent years.

To make sure they do not get stuck in their own webs, spiders also spin unsticky threads. They then walk carefully across the unsticky parts.

There are a few animals who have a tiger and a lion for parents. They are called tigons.

Some prairie dogs are big smoochers. Those that live in the same colony evidently greet each other with a kiss and a few brushes of the nose.

A blue whale's tongue weighs the same as three dozen people.

The porcupine quill is really made of hair. The hairs have grown together to form stiff sharp swords.

Moss does not always grow on the north side of a tree. It will form on the side with the least sunlight. Often that is the north side.

Approximately 2,000 meteors hit the earth every day. A meteor hit Arizona and left a hole 575 feet deep. That is deeper than the Washington Monument is high.

Miracles were recorded in the Bible so that you will believe that the man Jesus is the Son of God.

"Jesus' disciples saw him do many other miracles besides the ones told about in this book, but these are recorded so that you will believe that he is the Messiah, the Son of God, and that believing in him you will have life" (John 20:30, 31).

1. Name two unusual facts you learned about nature.
2. What are two miracles in the Bible?
3. Why do you think Jesus performed miracles?

twelve

Getting Away

Suppose you want to get away from a friend. You can hide behind a tree; you can outrun him or take a different path. Many times animals need to get away from danger, and some creatures have amazing ways to escape.

One of the most unusual ways to get away is the method used by several lizards, like the green anole. If a bird sweeps down and grabs this reptile by the tail, the green anole will simply drop its tail. The surprised bird will be left hanging there disappointed while the lizard runs away.

You might feel sorry for the green anole, but don't worry too much about it. If left in peace, this lizard will begin growing a new tail for another bird or snake to pull off.

Lizards are not the only creatures that have great ways to escape danger.

Another great getaway artist is the snowshoe hare. It looks much like a rabbit and lives in cold areas of the North. Its first trick is the ability to change colors to fit the season. When conditions are extremely cold, the snowshoe has white hair and travels across the snow as if it were a ghost. However, when the temperature warms up and the daylight appears for more hours, this hare turns a shade of brown.

Despite its ability to change colors, life is still dangerous for the snowshoe. Often its best chance to survive is to run. That is when its big feet come in handy. Its feet are 4 to 6 inches long, which is very large for its size. Oversized feet allow them to run across the top of snow at speeds up to 25 miles per hour. Many of their enemies merely sink into the snow with each step. While the hunting animal is stuck in deep snow, the snowshoe goes bouncing across the top, sometimes reaching nearly 12 feet with each bound.

There are many ways to avoid danger, but often the best way is simply to run. Some situations become very threatening if you stay around just to see what will happen.

If you see some young people shoplifting, the best thing to do is to get out of there as quickly as you can. Some people have stayed to watch and have been arrested with the shoplifters.

When others decide to experiment with drugs, you know exactly what to do. Look for the nearest exit and don't look back. Those who are "just curious" could end up in a lot of trouble.

Running away from trouble is sometimes the best thing to do. If necessary, say no, but definitely aim your feet for the door.

"Run from anything that gives you the evil thoughts that young men often have, but stay close to anything that makes you want to do right" (2 Tim. 2:22).

1. How does the green anole lizard escape danger?
2. How does the snowshoe hare escape danger?
3. How can young people escape an invitation to do wrong?

thirteen

Fathers Make a Difference

You can find all sorts of fathers in nature: everything from fathers who raise their own young, to dads who have absolutely nothing to do with them. Some make excellent parents who share duties and prove patient and caring with their babies.

For instance, who takes the youngsters for rides in the poison dart frog family? The father is the one who packs junior on his back and gives him a trip to the local pond.

And who enjoys wrestling with baby baboon? It's the father

39

who gets down in the dirt and tumbles around. His presence seems to calm the small ones down and allows the family to get along in relative peace.

This is not to say that mothers do not play important roles in nature. Generally speaking they do more than their share of the work. However, in some species the male parent carries out his responsibilities just as well.

The emu is a prime example of father care. The fathers devote two years to the process of training their chicks. They give special instruction in searching for food and in the art of dodging enemies.

Father wolf takes his job seriously, too. Not only does he hunt for food for the family but he teaches his pups to do the same. He is not content to push his young out into the world but takes time to train them. This is true of several of the more intelligent species.

Sandpipers seem to designate most of the food gathering chores to father. He assumes the baby chicks are his and not the mother's, since she lays eggs for several males. The females appear to be continuously in the process of producing eggs and evidently have little time to visit the supermarket.

The Siamese fighting fish is a proud and hard working father. He builds a nest out of bubbles. Each bubble is thick because it is made from mucus. Father constructs this nest near the surface of the water and places eggs from the female inside. While they are waiting to hatch, the Siamese keeps a close guard over the eggs. He remains near in case any danger threatens. Not content to leave his eggs to chance, this parent wants to help usher them into this world.

Not all of us are fortunate enough to have a father living with us, but those who are have good reason to thank God. Fathers, like mothers, can be very caring and can help us do things. They are often fun to be with.

Few things make a father happier than when his children grow up showing good common sense. Children who avoid trouble as much as possible, who learn to handle responsibility and try to follow God, bring fathers a great deal of happiness.

It feels good to have a father around with whom you can share time and do things together. Thank God for your father if you have one. If you don't, then God has promised to be a special father to you, and you can thank Him for that.

"My son, how I will rejoice if you become a man of common

sense. Yes, my heart will thrill to your thoughtful, wise words"
(Prov. 23:15, 16).

1. What does the Siamese fighting fish build his nest from?
2. Name two animal fathers and what they do for their children.
3. Name one trait that makes a good dad.

fourteen

Ants Keep Livestock

If you want to study nature, you don't have to travel to foreign lands. You won't have to climb a snow-capped mountain or descend into a huge canyon. You can spend many happy hours sitting on the ground, watching ants go about their lives. Ants do far more interesting things than most people realize.

Take for instance the dairy ant. You can call it that because it actually keeps other insects in order to use their "milk." They keep livestock, feed them, protect them and live off the little creatures.

The livestock are called aphids, small lice that live on plants. Usually people try to get rid of them because they feed off the plant juices. The tiny aphid has two small tubes leading from its body. From those tubes ants are able to take a sweet tasting liquid. The ants enjoy the healthy "honeydew."

Somehow in their insect world the aphid and the ant work out a deal that both enjoy. The ants build a house for the aphids. They are protected there and allowed to carry on their daily tasks. In turn, the aphids serve as dairy cows for the ants.

No one knows how the ant figured out this system or why the aphids first trusted the ant. However, it has gone on for many centuries. The ant builds a structure out of string-like plant parts. After the ant has woven a "barn" or "shed," the aphids happily move into their new home.

Several species of ants have learned to milk aphids. There are probably some "dairies" in your yard, since they can be found most places.

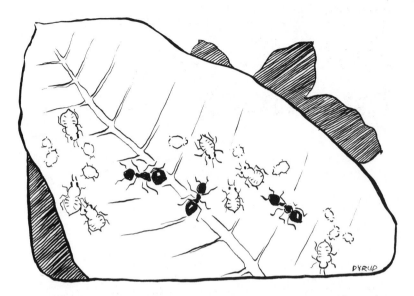

If you have carpenter ants, watch them climbing branches that are covered with tiny insects. The carpenter ant will gently stroke the aphid with its antennae. Feeling relaxed and comfortable the aphid gives off a pleasant tasting liquid which the ant is happy to drink.

Because aphids are important to ants, they are generally treated well. The ant makes sure plenty of food, housing and protection are provided.

If you visit Mexico you can see a similiar sight with caterpillars rather than aphids. Here not only do the ants keep the blue butterfly larva in pens but at night they take the caterpillars out to graze. The ants lead the caterpillars to croton plants to feed. When they are done, the ants return them to their pens.

The ants milk these creatures for their honeydew in the same way the aphids are used.

Ants would be foolish to ignore the aphids that provide food, just as we would be silly to leave milk out on the table to spoil or forget to place meat in the refrigerator. Smart people take care of the things that are important to them.

Too often we throw away half an apple or we toss out a box of cereal before it is empty. How many times have we poured more milk into a glass than we are able to drink?

God is concerned that we take good care of the things we have. If we are wasteful and thoughtless, we could end up having to do without. Ants watch over the aphids because they need them. People need to be just as careful with the things they consider valuable.

"For the man who uses well what he is given shall be given more, and he shall have abundance. But from the man who is unfaithful, even what little . . . he has shall be taken from him" (Matt. 25:29).

1. Describe the dairy ant and its livestock.
2. What are some things you do to be careful about not wasting?
3. Could you go for one month without buying anything new and instead fix up and use what you already have?

fifteen

Why Finches Don't Freeze

Any self-respecting bird should have enough sense to fly south in the winter. However, many of our feathered friends prefer snow instead of the beach. They can be found perched in leafless trees in parks, forests and backyards all over the North.

The key question to scientists is, How do birds keep from freezing to death in such cold climates? Some birds die during the winter, but many others survive quite well.

Like people, birds have learned to adapt to the frigid North. Each variety has developed its own ingenious system. A few birds put on winter coats by growing a thicker layer of feathers. Some find excellent shelters and build their homes protected from the terrible winds.

Other birds, like the finch, look within themselves for the extra heat needed to survive. The finch shivers to keep warm with its tiny heart beating 500 times a minute! Shivering isn't too difficult to understand. That is exactly what you and I do when our bodies try to fight against the cold.

When we shiver, our body muscles contract to produce body heat. Without our external frame moving, the inside of our physical machine moves to create warmth.

The small finch loses heat quickly because it has a little body. Large birds can stay warm longer and can skip meals if necessary. Finches are not so fortunate. In order for them to shiver so much they must constantly find food. Food supplies the fuel that allows their muscles to contract or move. It is the contracting muscles that supply heat.

In some of the worst weather the finch is able to stay comfortable inside. It supplies its own heat and therefore can survive.

When human beings face tough times, they often need to find strength from inside. A teacher yells at them. The neighbor's dog chases them. A mean kid takes the ball and throws it on the roof. Life can be cold and hard.

God understands that some days are rough. This is one of the reasons He decided to send the Holy Spirit to live inside of us. The Holy Spirit makes us feel better, calms us down and becomes our constant comforter.

On days when things seem to go wrong, we can remember that God has not left us alone. He has given us the Holy Spirit to help us—from the inside.

"But when the Father sends the Comforter instead of me— and by the Comforter I mean the Holy Spirit—he will teach you much, as well as remind you of everything I myself have told you" (John 14:26).

1. Name ways birds adapt to cold weather.
2. How does a finch keep warm?
3. How does God help us face tough times?

sixteen

How Much Wood Does a Woodchuck Chuck?

The famous tongue twister asks the question, "How much wood would a woodchuck chuck if a woodchuck could chuck wood?" There's no easy answer to that one since a woodchuck doesn't chuck wood. In fact, it isn't even a woodchuck; it is a groundhog. Early Americans misunderstood the Indian name for the groundhog, and many of us have been misnaming it ever since.

Those who did get the name correct decided the groundhog was a good weatherman. That is why we have the story that if a groundhog sees its shadow on February 2 in Punxsutawney, Pennsylvania, winter will last six more weeks. Actually, this date is too early for any sane groundhog to poke its nose out.

If a groundhog has its way, it will spend most of the day digging and eating. By fall it hopes to be stuffed so it can sleep or hibernate through the winter. They are not accustomed to storing food for the frozen season. Overeating is closer to their style.

To carry out their favorite hobby of eating, they have a great set of teeth. Much of their day is spent grinding down vegetation.

Life is not always peaceful for our furry friend. For one thing groundhogs can be fairly rough on each other. One or two tend to take over and are soon telling everyone else what to do.

A more serious problem is the fox. Faster and perhaps smarter than the groundhog, the fox frequently cuts down groundhog numbers. The danger presented by the fox may be the reason the groundhog often sits upright, looking alertly around. However, when it does this, it is left wide open for human hunters. A groundhog sitting on its back legs makes it a perfect target for gunshots.

Living underground has definite advantages. A groundhog's apartment has both front and back doors. It needs two entrances in case a fox makes it uncomfortable. While the fox snoops at one door, the groundhog is gone out the other. Some burrows have half a dozen entrances or more.

Called a burrow, the living quarters drop 6 feet beneath the surface and wind around for 45 feet. There are several rooms where different members can either hide or hibernate.

To provide this type of housing groundhogs spend a great deal of time digging. They remove hundreds of pounds of dirt in order to construct a home. Fortunately they carry their own earth-moving equipment. Their front legs serve as diggers while their hind feet throw the dirt out of the hole. Their front feet have especially sharp claws.

Because of their need to dig, groundhogs have been disliked for centuries. When a farmer's prize cow steps into a groundhog's hole and injures its leg, the farmer may become furious.

Despite its unpopularity the groundhog must continue to dig. Otherwise it will have no place to raise its family. At the same time the farmer cannot have the invader tearing up his place.

Constant diggers will never be popular. Neither will people who keep digging into the personal lives of others. Some of us like to dig up dirt about others. We like to hear gossip and spread stories that make others look bad.

God wants us to stay away from dirt digging. We can help each other far more if we say nice things rather than spread ugly stories about other human beings.

"An ungodly man diggeth up evil, and in his lips there is as a burning fire" (Prov. 16:27, KJV).

1. What is the correct name for a woodchuck?
2. What is the main enemy of the groundhog?
3. Describe a groundhog home.

seventeen

Even Lions Get the Blues

What kind of troubles could a lion have? They're huge beasts that can leap across two cars and take most animals down. Lions seem to lead peaceful lives. It isn't often that any creature wants to start a fight with one of these giant, muscular cats.

Female lions are able to spend much of their time lying near water holes, playing with their cubs. Cubs enjoy pulling at each other, chewing on mother's tail and pushing one another around. Sometimes they get a bit too rough and tempers flare.

Lions like the feeling of closeness. When it sleeps, a lion often has a paw or its head up against another lion. Meeting in the open, they like to rub heads. Generally, lions live in extended families called prides. The group will consist of five or more females, their cubs and usually one adult male. Some lions travel in pairs but most want to join prides.

Most of the time lions look like they're on vacation. Lying around and sleeping is their idea of a great day. If they could read newspapers they would be just like many human parents on Sunday afternoons. Often they spend as little as four hours a day doing any real activity.

It isn't easy to keep a lion's stomach full. A single meal for an adult male may consist of 50 pounds of meat. The lioness is smaller and often makes a better hunter than the male. However, hunting isn't the only way to acquire food. Lions can turn into first-class bullies. If another type of animal has brought game down, the lion will move in and force the original hunter away.

Since the lion is the king of the beasts, one would think lions have it made. However, life can not only be tough for the lion, but it can also be extremely dangerous.

One of the big troubles a lion faces is drought. If no rain comes, both water and food become scarce. Some of the animals that lions hunt starve to death. Others wander miles away to find food. This in turn causes the lion to travel to support itself and its cubs. Desperate for food, a few lions do starve.

Even in good weather lions have trouble finding food. Many of the animals they hunt are decreasing in numbers, causing hardship on the pride.

When a lion finds a prey, it is by no means certain to catch it. A lion might chase 20 animals before it is able to catch one. If it happens to catch a small animal, it may have to share that meal with ten other lions. There is no end to the shopping they need to do.

It would look like a lion is in control during a chase, but that isn't always the case. A prey will try to run away from a lion, naturally, but if the cat gets close, he might get kicked. Many lions lose an eye or some teeth or get broken bones from trying to take down an animal. When a lion is wounded, it has to take time to heal. During that time it's nearly impossible to find food.

All of us have troubles. Even if you were the king of the beasts, on some days things would be rough. No matter how old you are, you will always face troubles once in a while.

We need to give our problems to someone else to handle for us. Unlike lions, we can take them to Christ and ask Him to help us with them. When we do, God hears us and helps us through our troubles.

"I am radiant with joy because of your mercy, for you have listened to my troubles and have seen the crisis in my soul" (Ps. 31:7).

1. What is a pride and what does it consist of?
2. What are some troubles a lion faces?
3. How can Christ help you when you face troubles?

eighteen

Squirrels are Acrobats

If you have squirrels living in your backyard, you are a fortunate person. You don't have to hike for miles into the forest to see nature at its best. The squirrels have brought the back country to your doorstep.

Squirrels are one of the best shows in town, too. Without spending a dime you can sit inside your living room and watch their crazy antics.

They are excellent at climbing trees and leaping from one branch to another. Have you ever watched two squirrels chasing each other through the trees? They move so quickly they are hard to follow, but you can certainly hear the noise as they rattle the leaves and tear along. In a flash they can switch branches or reverse direction and be gone again.

While you are watching the squirrel in your yard or in the local park, ask yourself some questions about its behavior. How does a squirrel get up onto a bird feeder? The little rodent must know it is stealing food, but how can it get up a straight metal pole? Do your squirrels ever climb onto the telephone wires? Some are such good acrobats that they can tightrope walk. They can also leap from tree to tree using their bushy tails to balance their flight.

If you want to see a champion acrobat, you have to find a flying squirrel. Actually they do more hang gliding than flying, but they do travel through the air. However, they are pretty much restricted to night flights.

As a good investigative scientist, you will also want to take note of where your squirrels live. This one could be tricky. Do your squirrels live in the hollow of a tree? They are likely to live in trees until the weather gets nice. Squirrels will then often build summer homes in the form of nests. Check to see if you can find both bird nests and squirrel nests in your yard.

No study would be complete without checking out the squirrels' food supply. They have two pressing jobs to keep up with. The first one is to find enough food to eat each day and the second is to store up meals for the winter.

Generally speaking, squirrels collect nuts. They also enjoy a large selection of corn, wheat and fruit.

If you watch closely you might be able to see the fast-fingered little creature burying its cache in the ground. It will spend a great deal of time storing up for tomorrow, and the squirrel is wise to do it. Later, it will have an amazing ability to find that exact spot and dig up the food, even if it is buried under the snow. How does a squirrel do it? Can it smell the nuts buried there? Does it somehow recognize the scenery? Has its mind marked off the area in some mathematical dimension? We don't know, but God knows.

Storing up so we can have food for tomorrow is a solid principle people are smart to follow. The bad thing is that some people spend all of their time collecting goods for tomorrow. They forget to share the things they have with people who need them.

Jesus seemed concerned over people who are capable of gathering things only for themselves. He encouraged us to share our possessions with others.

"Don't store up treasures here on earth where they can erode away or may be stolen. Store them in heaven where they will never lose their value, and are safe from thieves. If your profits are in heaven your heart will be there too" (Matt. 6:19–21).

1. Where do squirrels live in winter? In summer?
2. Where do squirrels store their food?
3. How do we store up treasure in heaven?

nineteen

Sheep Living in the Mountains

Not all sheep live on level pastures with rolling green fields. Many wander among high mountain ranges and almost tiptoe across dangerous cliffs. They leap over rocks where one false step would lead to certain death. And despite their excellent ability, some do fall and are injured or killed.

Their experience and knowledge of rough mountains becomes one of their better defenses. If they are attacked by a bear, coyote, wolf, eagle or other predator, the mountain sheep will head directly for the most dangerous part of the cliffs. There they will climb around on the most treacherous rocks to discourage their attacker.

Since sheep cannot speak for themselves, we can only guess why they choose to live in the mountains. However, some of the benefits of mountain living seem obvious.

Sheep remain within easy strolling distance of small mountain fields of lush grass. And yet when the need arises, they can scurry to the safety of the rugged terrain close by.

Generally speaking, water is no problem at these heights. Some mountains have snow nearly year round. As it melts, the snow furnishes beautiful streams and lakes.

With all of their assets mountain ranges are not without their problems. When the severe winter sets in, many sheep perish from the harsh elements. Newborn lambs frequently fail to live through their first winter.

Many lambs like to play with each other. They will butt heads and jump over rocks. And sometimes they drift away from the older sheep as they play. Quietly a coyote may watch them in hopes that they will stray too far and it can cut them off from the others and add them to its diet.

Fortunately, most lambs begin to sense the danger and realize they have strayed. Quickly and safely they hustle after the others and the protection there is in numbers.

The Bible repeatedly describes us as being like sheep. We stray away from God. And when we stray we sin or do things that are wrong. Fortunately, Jesus has died to pay for all our sins. We have strayed, but we are welcomed back into the presence of God because Jesus died for us.

"We are the ones who strayed away like sheep! We, who left God's paths to follow our own. Yet God laid on him the guilt and sins of every one of us!" (Isa. 53:6).

1. Why do sheep like to live in mountains?
2. How is water supplied in the mountains?
3. How are people like sheep?

twenty

Monkeys with Large Noses

As we grow up we begin to look at ourselves and often we do not like our appearance. We stand in front of a mirror and we stare at our nose or we start to think our ears are too big. We may not even like our chin, our hair, our eyes or some other feature. Almost all young people go through a time of disliking something about their face.

If a young person were a proboscis monkey he would have a serious problem. This monkey comes into the world with a small nose, but soon it begins to grow rapidly. By the time it is full grown its nose is so long and wide that it covers part of the monkey's mouth. Sometimes it has to push its nose aside in order to eat.

No one has found out how the monkey feels about this large member of its body, but it could be that it likes it. Maybe other monkeys think this is the best-looking nose in all of nature.

We do know that the proboscis makes good use of its prominent nose. It uses it as a very loud horn. If another monkey moves into its territory, the proboscis gives a couple of loud bursts through its nose. That sound sends a message telling others they had better clear out quickly.

The proboscis monkey is hard to find outside of zoos. Far-off Borneo is the only place they can be found in the wild. Borneo is located approximately halfway between Australia and Asia. Living in a hot climate, one of its favorite recreations is to take a swim in a local river to cool off.

None of us looks like a proboscis monkey. Most of us have

normal features that we can easily be happy with. As we grow older we usually stop worrying about ears and noses because we realize how little they really mean. Honesty is more important than dimples. Love means more than curly hair. Friends are more valuable than dark eyebrows.

Frequently the very feature that bothers you is something that others find fantastic. Brown eyes are beautiful. Blue eyes are terrific. Hazel eyes are friendly.

Ancient King Solomon looked at the woman he loved and told her that her nose was like the tower of Lebanon. Solomon was one of the wisest men who ever lived and he adored the good-sized nose on the woman he loved.

Our features are not ugly. They are simply parts of a very interesting person.

"Your nose is shapely like the tower of Lebanon overlooking Damascus" (Song of Sol. 7:4).

1. What does a proboscis monkey use his nose for?
2. Where does the proboscis monkey live?
3. What would you tell someone who thinks he is ugly?

twenty-one

When Elephants Get Thirsty

When an elephant wants a drink of water, it has a big problem. An animal that big can't get by on a few sips from a puddle. A good drink of cold water on a hot day might mean 35 gallons of water. (Try to imagine yourself drinking 35 gallons of milk at the table tonight.)

Since the world is 70 percent water, you may think there would be no trouble finding plenty to drink. However, many people and animals die each year because there is not enough water to raise crops or to drink.

There are many reasons why some people do not have enough water. It may have been too hot in that land for too long so that ponds evaporated. There may not have been much rain and the rivers dried up. Possibly there has been war and people are not free to move around to get water.

Elephants not only need water to keep their insides working, but they must get huge amounts of water for their outsides. An elephant is a gigantic physical machine. On a hot day it is easy for this machine to overheat. Human bodies can overheat also. That is why we drink water, perspire, take cool baths and look for shady places. Sometimes, we may overheat and get sick.

To stay healthy elephants look for a good watering hole. Ideally they want to find enough water to stand in and take a shower. They carry an excellent shower hose with them. Their trunk can suck up a large supply of water. The elephant then points the hose over its back and lets the water gush.

Mother elephants like to help out their young. That's why

59

they spray their children with a short shower, too. As the small ones grow they get better at showering themselves.

In dry areas the search for water is a constant problem. Elephants wander in small herds from hole to hole looking for more. If they run out of places to look, the elephants turn to another plan. They begin digging holes in the ground in search of water.

Not very adept at using shovels, a desperate elephant will use practically any part of its body to dig. Tusks, trunk and feet each become valuable tools in its search for water.

Finally the elephant will find a small collection of water or at least some soggy mud. Their determination to find water is the only reason some of these huge machines survive.

As long as we live, the need for water will control our lives. Both animals and people dare not wander too far from this valuable liquid. We can go much longer without food than we can without water.

When Jesus spoke to a woman at a well, He offered her living water. He told her she would never be thirsty again; He promised her eternal life. Eternal life would be like having a spring inside her and she would never run out of water.

Eternal life never runs out. Jesus lived and died so that you could believe in Him and live forever. You will never run out of life—even after you die.

" 'But the water I give them,' he said, 'becomes a perpetual spring within them, watering them forever with eternal life' " (John 4:14).

1. How much water does an elephant drink on a hot day?
2. Why do some parts of the world not have enough water?
3. What did Jesus say about water?

twenty-two

Fur Coat for Your House

Last year we painted our house. Before we applied the paint, we spent many days scraping the wood. We even sanded down the front door. After we had scraped the wood, we could see all the problems it had.

Some of the wood had termite damage we needed to repair. Other places had nicks where things had bumped the building over the years. In other areas the wood had become stained or rotted because of the weather. We spent a lot of days trying to repair the damage to the building.

A few scientists believe we are putting the wrong material on houses. They would like to see a company manufacture artificial fur. It would be like fitting a gigantic fur coat over your house.

Before you laugh too loudly, you should know that there are scientists who are experimenting with this idea. They came up with the idea by studying polar bears. A polar bear's fur is excellent at trapping heat from the sun and carrying warmth into the animal's skin.

That ability is precisely why a polar bear looks white. Its fur is not really white but only looks that way. When photographed with a special camera, we can see the bear as black.

Consequently, a professor has worked hard at trying to create a thread that acts like the hair of a polar bear. He would like to lay that fake fur on the roof of a house and possibly spread a little more around the sides of the building. The fake hair would collect rays from the sun and carry warmth into the house.

So far the government hasn't become excited about fur coats for houses. They do not want to give money to experiment in the overcoat business.

But if some material like this could be developed, it could serve two purposes. It would keep homes warm and it would hide the nicks, cuts, dents and stains that we now see on houses. We could cover them like we cover old furniture.

This is what God does when He covers our sins. We have each done things that have been wrong. That is a fact that will not go away. But God is willing to cover our sins with His love. Then our sins are gone. God does not see them anymore because He has forgiven them.

God reaches out and covers us with His love through Jesus Christ. He forgives us of all our sins.

"And forgiven the sins of your people—yes, covered over each one" (Ps. 85:2).

1. Where does the idea of a fur coat for your house come from?
2. How can we have our sins covered over?

twenty-three

Marmots Like to Play

It would be interesting to make a list of how many animals enjoy playing: otters, kittens, dolphins, foxes and all kinds of cubs and pups. You could probably add others. One creature who takes time out for fun is the marmot.

This little rodent leads a short, rugged, dangerous life. With that kind of pressure it needs to find ways to relax.

Its name comes from French and means "mountain mouse." If you ever take the cog railroad up Pikes Peak in Colorado, you will probably see them sitting along the rocks staring at the strange tourists riding the train.

Although their name means mouse, marmots can grow to become good-sized. They might weigh up to 25 pounds. Their front teeth, long hair and full tails give them the appearance of beavers.

The Olympic marmots of Olympic National Park in Washington state are often called "whistle pigs" because of the security system they have adopted. When a colony of marmots is outside its burrow, one of the members serves as a sentry. It watches the area for any possible enemies.

Marmots do not lack for enemies. Hawks, eagles, mountain lions and coyotes would all like to include a marmot in their daily menu. If the sentry sights one of these creatures or any other likely intruder, it gives off a whistle designed to startle the deepest sleeper.

Hurriedly the marmots race for the safety of their homes and wait for the predators to leave. Predators are anything which destroy or eat animals. Many animals are predators.

Even without enemies the marmot has a rough life. The winters are snow-packed and many do not survive winter's hibernation. Because of the cold in their high altitudes, marmots can spend a mere five months in the open air.

But no one has ever heard the marmots complain. They are too busy getting the most out of life. Marmots love lying in the sun catching a few "rays." They seem to enjoy their friends and the other marmots that live in their colony.

When time allows, they like to find other marmots and wrestle in the grass. In friendly play two of them will rise up on their back legs and lock arms. If possible they will tussle until one tosses its opponent into the twigs. He then gets up and happily goes at it again.

Life can be harsh for all of us. We don't have predators looking for us, but there is sickness, disaster, disappointment and failure. When time allows we ought to get in some playfulness. God gave us a sense of humor and the ability to laugh. It would be a shame to waste it.

"And Sarah declared, 'God has brought me laughter! All who hear about this shall rejoice with me' " (Gen. 21:6).

1. What is a predator?
2. Tell about the sentry system the Olympic marmots have.
3. What activity do marmots have that we should copy?

twenty-four

The Arctic Fox

How much of your day is spent looking for food? Most of us can find food in one of two places, either our kitchen or at the local store. Usually animals do not have life this easy. Many have to move from place to place in a constant search for food.

The arctic fox is a good example of a constant food shopper. Food becomes scarce in the cold arctic areas with temperatures dropping to –60°F. or less. To survive, the fox has grown a long fur coat. It comes in a fluffy white to help the fox hide against the frozen background.

Not every arctic fox goes south to escape the cold. The southern areas are filled with danger. There are many animals and people who love to hunt this lovely little creature. A number of arctic fox will travel north to within 50 miles of the North Pole.

The desire to survive may drive this animal 1,000 miles and back again. The fox is in a dangerous position. If it stays put, it may soon run out of food. If it moves around, it is likely to become a victim to human or nonhuman hunters. Consequently many arctic foxes never return home again.

Moving north would seem like certain death, but the fox often manages to survive. The land is frozen with practically no plant or animal life. A tough and smart creature, this fox turns up food in places where it is hard to imagine.

If you want to be a scientist, studying the arctic fox would be a challenge few others have tried. You might find it interesting to figure out how the fox finds food near the Arctic.

They aren't picky eaters because they can't afford to be. It is believed they can find food buried several feet under the ice. Frozen conditions have forced them to learn how to wait for food. A fox can dig a hole in the ice and place its snow-white body into the space. When a small animal comes by, the fox lunges out against its victim.

Fortunately, an arctic fox carries extra body fat and can go up to three weeks without food. However, it cannot go forever. They eat birds that did not go south. Eggs are a favorite delicacy for this hunger.

At night the arctic fox can hear the noisy shifting of ice floes. Floe pushing against floe sounds as loud as a freight train near the top of the world.

Traveling close to the water, this fox is happy to eat dead sea animals that have washed ashore. Seals and whales are likely to become part of their diet.

In the spring those foxes that survive return to their home areas. Many have died but others have won at the challenging game of searching for food.

Nature can be harsh. That is why many of us feed birds during the winter or leave water outside for dogs and cats.

Life can be just as cruel to human beings. Millions of people live in a continuous search for food. They scrape through garbage cans. Some beg on the streets for food. Many babies die for lack of milk and food.

Jesus knew we would always have hungry, even starving, people with us. That is why He taught us to feed those who are starving.

It is a shame that animals must starve. How much worse that some people cannot find enough to eat.

"For I was hungry and you fed me; I was thirsty and you gave me water; I was a stranger and you invited me into your homes" (Matt. 25:35).

1. What color is the arctic fox?
2. What is one of the hardest jobs for the arctic fox?
3. What has your family done to help starving people?

twenty-five

The Mighty Amazon

Do you like adventure? Would you enjoy traveling on a river filled with dangerous fish? How about seeing hundreds of thousands of insects, many of which have never been named? Would you like to ride a boat 4,000 miles without ever leaving the same river? Do you mind terribly high humidity where all day long you are dripping wet?

If you answered yes to these questions, you may be ready to explore the famous Amazon River. Located in South America, it is born in the high Peruvian Andes. Winding its way across massive Brazil, the Amazon finally pours its cargo into the mighty Atlantic Ocean.

Before you buy a plane ticket and head for the jungles of Amazonia, you should know what to expect. Take a camera along in case you spot a dolphin arching out of the freshwater river. And don't forget to keep your hands in the boat in case your boat rides over some piranhas. A long blade machete will come in handy if you decide to walk into the jungle. Most of the area is so seldom traveled that it is nearly impossible to make your way through the thick overgrowth.

There is no need to worry about being lonely even during the night. The insects would not think of leaving you alone. You won't need a radio because the monkeys are willing to chat with you all night long. Monkeys will also keep you company during the day with their bright colored faces and circus tricks.

If you are tired of garter snakes in your backyard, you will be surprised at the reptiles that crowd the jungle. The anaconda, possibly the world's longest snake at 30 feet in length, would be pleased to meet you. Bushmasters are smaller snakes which are attracted to a human's body heat. Snakes find the jungle a good place to live and raise their children.

Under almost ideal conditions large, beautiful trees have prospered along the Amazon. Prized varieties such as cedar stretch majestically toward heaven. Trees provide homes for an almost endless number of animals. Some of the trees are decked with gorgeous orchids growing freely on their trunks.

As you move lazily along the river and drink in some of its wonders, your mind might think of Psalm 1:3. The verse speaks of those who follow God. Christians are like the healthy, towering trees by the river. Their lives are full and satisfying because "they delight in doing everything God wants them to do."

"They are like trees along a river bank bearing luscious fruit each season without fail. Their leaves shall never wither, and all they do shall prosper" (Ps. 1:3).

1. Where is the Amazon River located?
2. Name some animals found in that region?
3. How are Christians like trees, according to Psalm 1?

twenty-six

How Smart Are You?

When we go to school and study with other students, we soon wonder how smart we are. Before long we compare ourselves with the others in the class. Some people do their math faster than you do. But you may write better sentences than someone else in the class.

Soon you find out that you may be smart in one subject and not as smart in another. Some will learn that they have trouble remembering stories but they are good at working with machines. They are smart at different things.

God made people so they would be intelligent in one way or another. An animal might be very smart in one thing and not as smart in another. But God definitely made you smart.

An arctic tern can't read a book but it can do some things that most people can't do. Arctic terns leave home at the age of six weeks, fly 11,000 miles from home and return next summer to the same nesting area. In navigation a tern is extra smart.

Some people argue that the dolphin is nature's most intelligent animal outside of man. Dolphins do seem to have talents for language that are very unusual. They have little difficulty talking to each other and are able to learn a vocabulary as well as grammar. A dolphin may not be able to fly a plane, but a dolphin is still smart.

Bees aren't dummies either. When a bee tells its fellow bees where to find nectar, the message needs to be correct. By special dancing the bee tells its friends what direction to fly and exactly how far to go. And yet bees in another county might not be able to understand the language of this particular bee. Some scientists believe a bee's language is the most complicated in the world outside of human beings.

It's true that a bee can't fill out an income tax form, but a bee is still smart. Bees understand something about geometry. The hives they build are often made of little sections created at precise mathematical angles.

All of us are smart, one way or another. And because we are smart we are able to think about God and what He means to us. We aren't smart enough to totally understand God, but we

71

are intelligent enough to think about Him and to believe in Him.

When we think of how much He loves us, we think about how much He cares and we realize how close God is to us.

Because we can think about God, we are able to come to Him and believe in His Son Jesus Christ.

"I thought about the wrong direction in which I was headed, and turned around and came running back to you" (Ps. 119:59, 60).

1. What special ability does an arctic tern have?
2. What special ability does a dolphin have?
3. What special ability does a bee have?
4. What special ability do you have?

twenty-seven

The Skunk Pig

The next time you're in the Texas, Arizona, New Mexico area, take a ride around and look for the javelina (pronounced hava-leena). Weighing in at about 30 pounds, this short skunk pig can be found chewing on a local prickly pear.

Javelinas are neither skunks nor pigs, but they have reputations for acting like both. The only reason they remind people of skunks is their ability to give off a gagging odor. This terrible smell may not be given to frighten attackers, but it is strong enough to do the job. Its real purpose is probably to warn fellow javelinas to head for cover.

Their reputation for being pigs comes from merely one look at them. Javelinas have flat noses almost exactly like pig snouts. They have even developed grunts like pigs. Consequently, people in the area often call them "desert pigs."

If you study them more closely, the javelina turns out to be related to the boar. They can be found throughout Central and South America.

These little pig-like creatures probably got their names because of the sharp tusks that stick out of their mouths. To some the tusks looked like javelins. A running javelina was pictured as a menacing creature complete with a terrifying javelin, ready to run a person through.

Despite the terrible stories told about vicious javelina attacks, few if any of them are true. When a javelina sees a human being, it seems to have only one instinct—how to get away as quickly as possible. Sometimes they may have run past a person in an attempt to get away. Their quick escape may look like the charge of an ancient knight attacking with his long-handled spear. It is actually only a frightened animal looking for a way out.

With all of the study that has been done on the javelina, we

might expect some of the stories to go away. However, once an animal gets a bad reputation it takes hundreds of years for it to go away, if it ever stops. Many of the terrible things we believe about animals are simply not true. Most of the time we simply don't know any better.

A bad reputation is hard to correct. When someone lies, that is what we tend to remember about him. If someone steals something, we find that hard to forget.

The Bible tells us that dead flies will make something even as pleasant as perfume smell awful. In the same way, a very good person could do one bad thing and the bad thing will always be remembered.

Javelinas have bad reputations they do not deserve. Some people have bad reputations they do not deserve either. They may have made one mistake or two but that doesn't make them a bad person.

Often we need to forget something that a person has done and like him for the good person he is today.

"As dead flies give perfume a bad smell, so a little folly outweighs wisdom and honor" (Eccles. 10:1, NIV).

1. Why is the javelina called a skunk pig?
2. Where did the name javelina come from?
3. Do you know someone who has a bad reputation that you think doesn't deserve it? Explain.

74

twenty-eight

Swinging Monkeys

Do you ever wish you could travel through the trees like a monkey? Would you enjoy swinging from branch to branch going hundreds of yards without even touching the ground?

Not every monkey is at home flipping through the jungle, but a number of them seem to love it. Gibbons almost skip from tree to tree without stepping on the ground. They swing from branch to branch with such ease that they barely take time to touch each branch.

A few monkeys are so good at space travel, they use their tails to help them swing along. The spider monkey puts its tail to work like a fifth hand. Not only can he move quickly but his tail is so talented it can pick fruit just like a hand with fingers.

If a spider monkey should happen to tumble from a tree, its tail can reach out to rescue it. It will grasp a limb and immediately lock itself around the wood.

This tail is called prehensile. That means the tail is used as an extra limb or a fifth hand. When you visit the zoo watch to see which monkeys use their tails as extra limbs.

When a colobus monkey grows tired of tree living, it has a unique way of getting down. Like a fearless skydiver the colobus simply hurls itself into the air. Dropping a distance of a four-story building, the monkey merely spreads open its arms and legs. The colobus lands almost as gently as a butterfly.

Should you grow tired of regular monkeys, the ones that eat bananas and merely show off their teeth, take a trip to Asia. The Philippine macaque has developed a taste for seafood. It likes to hang around the water looking for fine food. When it becomes hungry enough, it will dive into the water and pull up a crab. Unafraid of its claws, the monkey has a feast.

While you visit the local zoo, ask yourself a couple of serious questions. Are you closely related to the monkeys and the apes that are housed there? Are they your closest relatives in nature?

None of the animals are really related to us. Some animals seem much more intelligent than the apes or monkeys. Some animals know far more about the world and navigation. They are better at building homes. Some animals can communicate better. A few are healthier. Even rodents and pigeons can perform some activities that chimpanzees cannot begin to comprehend.

Among God's creatures *man* is unique. There is no animal like us. And we are not like other animals. We see similarities between ourselves and most creatures, but we are not the same. God breathed life into human beings in a special way in order to make us His children.

"Then God said, 'Let us make a man—someone like ourselves, to be the master of all life upon the earth and in the skies and in the seas' " (Gen. 1:26).

1. What does prehensile mean?
2. How does a colobus monkey get down from a high spot?
3. What is the main difference between man and animals?

twenty-nine

How Good Is Your Memory?

Have you ever had trouble locating your books when it was time to go to school? Frantically you searched everywhere—behind the couch, in the closet, under the kitchen table. Finally you saw the stack and remembered that was exactly where you had left them.

Animals may not be as intelligent as humans, but some of them have amazing memories. Many animals can place food in the ground and find it months later just as if they carried a well-drawn map.

If you want to see an excellent memory at work, you could begin by watching a bird called the nutcracker. In September you can find them picking at pine cones in the western part of the United States. These pine cones begin to open in the fall season exposing their seeds. It looks like the pine tree wants birds to come along and take the seeds.

A nutcracker has a long bill and a small pouch. The bird eats as it works and also stuffs seeds into its pouch. It then flies away, often for miles, before reaching its hiding place.

When the nutcracker finds an area it likes, it pecks a small hole in the ground, a slender hole no more than an inch deep. The bird will deposit half a dozen seeds in its underground cupboard. The place is covered over and a tiny object is laid on the spot. A twig or a small stone will mark the spot. Working steadily, the nutcracker will bury many thousands of seeds in thousands of tiny holes.

Months later, often after a tough winter, a nutcracker is able to travel for miles and find the exact location of its seed deposits. Even though there are other stores of food around, the nut-cracker will find only the ones it hid.

A nutcracker's memory is not perfect, but it will find most of the seeds it buried. Fortunately, it does not find all of them because sometimes the seeds that are left in the ground become new pine trees.

These little birds cannot think the same way people think, but there is something remarkable about the memory God has given them. God knows that memories are important to both animals and people.

We don't get hit by cars because we remember to look both ways before we cross the street. We don't hit our heads if we remember to duck when we go through small places.

No one has a better memory than God himself. It is hard to imagine what life would be like if God forgot something. It would be terrible if one day He couldn't remember where He put the world.

Fortunately, God remembers each one of us. He remembers we are weak and He remembers to love us each day of our lives. God doesn't misplace people.

"He remembered our utter weakness, for his lovingkindness continues forever" (Ps. 136:23).

1. How does the nutcracker help the pine tree?
2. Tell how the nutcracker stores food.
3. Name one reason you are thankful for the memory God gives you.

thirty

Cleaning Animals

If you were an elephant and you needed a bath, you would have a big problem. A bathtub for elephants would be almost the size of a truck. Fortunately they don't need a tub. Elephants can take refreshing showers by using their trunks. They can also enjoy a hot dust bath. Throwing dust on themselves seems to get most insects off. Their next step is to use a tree for a towel. After a few rough brushes against a tree trunk, most small pests decide to leave the big bather alone.

Practically every creature finds some way to clean itself or finds something to clean it. If you have a birdbath in your yard, you have been able to watch your feathered friends freshen up on a hot day. Some birds enjoy baths so much that they will take them even while it's raining. On hot days they use the baths to cool off and to take a drink. If you want to draw birds into your yard, a feeder and a bath will help a great deal.

Families that have kittens for pets get to watch them take baths in a different way. For washcloths they use their tongues and paws to scrub their faces and even behind their ears. If they have a cat friend or parent, they often lick each other to help out at bath time.

Most animals are cleaner than we give them credit for. They spend much time grooming and washing. Frequently their idea of clean is different than ours, but looking good and feeling good is important in the world of nature.

Geckos are lizards that have a serious problem. They have no eyelids. What can they do if they get dirt in their eyes?

Fortunately geckos have long tongues that they use to clean out their eyes.

Baboons like to give each other dry baths. They do it by picking at each other to remove any matter that doesn't belong there. Sometimes they seem to groom each other merely for the pleasure of being near someone they like, much as children often comb their parents' hair.

Mice have reputations for being dirty and in some ways they certainly are. Some carry diseases that can be dangerous to human beings. Despite these problems they are personally extremely clean. Much of their spare time is dedicated to licking their paws and removing any leftover food or dirt.

People also are concerned about cleanliness. We spend a great deal of time keeping our bodies clean. Many of us spend enormous amounts of money to make sure we smell good.

The hardest part for man to reach and clean is his soul. We can't see or touch it. The only way we can reach the soul and cleanse it is to ask Jesus Christ to take care of the job.

"But if we confess our sins to him, he can be depended on to forgive us and to cleanse us from every wrong" (1 John 1:9).

1. How do elephants take baths?
2. How does a gecko lizard clean its eyes?
3. How does a person cleanse his soul from sin?

thirty-one

Dogs Are Friends

A friend of mine in Kansas had a black sheep dog with white spots. The dog had been trained to run out into a field and bring in 30 sheep all by itself. Dashing around the sheep, it could force them into a group and herd that group toward the corral. Sheep dogs have helped shepherds for centuries. They can be trained to take over a flock and control their behavior. Many dogs have worked for human beings in amazing ways.

In a small town in Nebraska a dog is credited with rescuing its owner. A lady was working at a dairy farm when a 1,600-pound Holstein bull struck her. As the woman tried to get away, the animal hit her twice more, throwing her into the air.

She had nearly passed out when suddenly her dog, a blue heeler, raced to her rescue. Familiar with livestock, the dog stood between the woman and the bull. Painfully she crawled under the fence and found help.

Dogs can be special friends and have frequently come to the aid of people in serious trouble. For years the famous St. Bernard dogs were used to help travelers in the Alps. A monastery at the Great St. Bernard Pass kept the dogs, and when a blizzard struck the area, they were sent out to find stranded victims. One dog, named Barry, is credited with saving over 40 people in a ten-year period.

In the 1960s a tunnel was dug through the Alps, so the St. Bernards are no longer needed as before. Usually the dogs are kept in the valley during the snowy season; however, they are still brought up to the monastery for the tourists to see.

Occasionally you will see a large, beautiful St. Bernard. Friendly and kind, they enjoy being with children and belonging to happy families.

Another dog that works as a friend to man is the handsome German shepherd. He makes a popular Seeing Eye dog because of his good common sense. A German shepherd has an excellent memory. A German shepherd is willing to do what he is told if he is trained properly. However, if you command a German shepherd to go forward and there is danger ahead, he will refuse to move. More than a guide dog, he is also capable of "thinking" through a situation.

Many dog trainers agree that if you want your dog to be your friend, the best way to train it is with kindness. Rewards, encouragement, gentleness and soft words let the animal know you really like it. When you like an animal, that animal is probably going to like you, too.

Dogs enjoy being around kind people. People want to be around kind people, too. Harshness, yelling, rudeness and anger chase others away. Kindness makes us fun to be around.

"Kindness makes a man attractive" (Prov. 19:22).

1. Name three ways that dogs are useful.
2. What special ability does a German shepherd have?
3. What is the best attitude if you want friends?

thirty-two

The Moose Is Back

In North America the moose population has grown to healthy numbers again. It's possible that no one is happier about that than God. He seems to show a real interest in preserving the creatures He has made.

Moose have had a tough time because of their size. As man keeps moving into the wilderness, there are fewer places for this stately animal to live. The adult male weighs 1,500 pounds and its antlers may stretch six feet across.

Natural enemies present plenty of danger to the moose. Black bears and wolves attack the calves and aged among the moose, thinning out their population.

In New England, a terrible threat to the moose is the tiny "brain worm." As thin as a line on paper, this small creature is mistakenly eaten by moose. The worm finds its way to the moose's brain and terrorizes the animal's nervous system. Soon they wander, confused and helpless, easy victims for winter, other animals and man.

Despite these problems man is a far greater enemy of the moose. If we hunt them without limitations, we tend to remove too many moose at the wrong time. Fortunately laws exist to control hunters from becoming carried away. These in turn help the hunter by guaranteeing that moose will be around to hunt in the future.

Another difficulty for the moose has been the destruction of protected park areas where they live. As man builds in these regions, the moose are forced to retreat into smaller sections

where they have difficulty in finding enough food.

However, as we stated at the beginning, this is a story of good news and not bad. The practices that had almost ruined the moose population have now turned around. The moose is making a comeback.

Fifty years ago the moose population in Maine had dropped to a mere 2,000. Today they have rebounded to an amazing 25,000. The Alaskan wilderness is home to an impressive 100,000.

Careful planning has demonstrated that there is room for both man and animals to live on this planet. Many animals now exist in record numbers and so do people. God is happy when man lives peaceably with animals. Animals provide food, clothing, companionship, and a sense of wonder to human beings. We must in turn provide territories where God's creatures can live and roam.

"Your righteousness is like the mighty mountains, your justice like the great deep. O Lord, you preserve both man and beast" (Ps. 36:6, NIV).

1. What are some enemies of the moose?
2. What is the good news for moose?
3. Do you think God is interested in preserving animals? Why do you think that?

thirty-three

Wild Horses

If you ever visit the mountains of Colorado, be sure to go horseback riding. We went recently with two young friends of ours, Josh and Jamie. Galloping up and down the hills and looking out across the valley from horseback is a great way to enjoy the outdoors.

Not every horse lives with people. There are still quite a few that run wild across the plains and mountains of America. Some of these horses have been turned loose by their owners. Others have run away from ranches. Many have come from parents and grandparents who have never been in captivity.

In our growing country some wonder how much longer horses

will be able to run wild. Other animals have been forced to retreat to high regions or have been practically killed off because man pushed too far.

Wild horses run in herds. The young male horses are called colts. Young females are fillies. Adult females are mares and adult males are stallions.

Among wild horse herds there is a definite order of leadership. Normally the commander is the stallion which runs at the rear of the herd. A mare will travel at the front as the second leader. The herd consists of mares and colts. When a colt becomes a stallion, he is usually forced by the leader to leave the herd. This places pressure on a stallion to collect some mares and in turn begin his own herd.

Many people envy the wild horse as they imagine them running freely across the fields. They may well be happy without the restraints of fences and corrals. Naturally it is a dangerous life since they could be destroyed by other animals, shot by man, injured by other horses or possibly starved to death. Some people would like to slaughter the horses for use as dog food and glue.

However, the freedom for the wild horses to run and even to struggle for themselves has been defended by many people. One of the most famous defenders of wild horses was a fifth-grade boy. This young boy led a fight to save the herds. Repeatedly he wrote to many congressmen describing the plight of wild

horses. Finally Congress passed a law protecting them. Today it is illegal to kill or otherwise hurt a horse living in the wild.

Refusing to be discouraged, this grade-school boy decided to get involved and help. Our society is filled with stories of young people who have spoken up and made a difference.

God realizes the value of young people and has often used them. They don't have to wait until they're adults or grow gray hair before they have anything worth saying. Today, young people are making a difference.

"Don't let anyone think little of you because you are young. Be their ideal; let them follow the way you teach and live; be a pattern for them in your love, your faith, and your clean thoughts" (1 Tim. 4:12).

1. What are the names for the following: a young male horse, a young female horse, an adult male horse, an adult female horse?
2. How did a fifth-grade boy help wild horses?
3. Tell about a young person whom you know and how he has shown his love for God.

thirty-four

Do Roadrunners Go "Beep Beep"?

When you watch cartoons, do you ever wonder if there really is a bird called a roadrunner? They may not look or act exactly like the ones on television but they certainly are real. If you wander onto the deserts of Texas and New Mexico, you might soon find yourself in a hot race with one of these fleet-footed characters.

At top speed the roadrunner hits 15 to 20 miles an hour. That divides into a mile every three minutes. Their running style is helped along by coasting through the air. Since they probably do not run too great a distance, they need to find ways of escape. Unafraid of the prickly cactus, they think nothing of scurrying in among the stickers to get away or to grab a quick bite of lunch.

Related to cuckoos, they stand less than one foot high and reach two feet in length. Their ability to race across the desert floor among the brush has caught the eye of thousands of amused onlookers.

In their hurry the roadrunner may be looking for a snack. A couple of juicy lizards will make its stomach feel good. If it gets lucky a baby rattlesnake is tasty. Insects make up a large part of their menu. A confident little creature, they do not hesitate to munch on mice and tarantulas. Their choice of delicacies helps considerably in keeping pest population under control.

It is unlikely that roadrunners actually make "beep beep"

noises. However, they are noisy. They make such a wide variety of sounds that you might wonder what's heading in your direction. By smacking its bill together in rapid motion, it can sound like a broken dinner bell.

They are good parents, for they go out in search of snake to feed their small family. Much of the roadrunners' time is spent gathering food.

Roadrunners hurry across the ground because they have a great deal to do. They move quickly to get food, to get back to their children, to avoid danger.

Most of us can move rapidly if there is something we really want to do. We hurry to catch planes, we hustle to birthday parties, we make a mad dash to kick a can. The writer of Psalms said he was in a hurry to get close to God. That was important to him. The sooner he could get it done, the better.

Some people are that way. They're in a hurry to learn more about God. They race to do what He wants. They move quickly to ask God for His help.

There are things in life that are worth chasing after. Getting close to God is something that should be done rapidly.

"The Lord is a strong fortress. The godly run to him and are safe" (Prov. 18:10).

1. How fast can roadrunners travel?
2. What is one of the many noises a roadrunner makes?
3. Name a couple of things you should hurry to do.

thirty-five

It's Cooler at the Beach

In the hot summer most of us like to spend a cool day at the beach. What is it that makes a lake, ocean or river a great place to be on a warm day?

If you stand near the water, you are often in the middle of a refreshing breeze. The sandy beach is hot. The air above that sand naturally goes up because hot air is lighter and moves upward. Just above the water there is cool air. As the hot air over the sand moves up, the cool air over the water moves in to take its place. The gentle wind you feel moving off the water is what we call a breeze. You feel much better because the temperature by the water is kept lower by the cool-air movement.

Not only does this happen next to the water, but you can often feel it half a mile away. If you are driving toward a lake you can frequently feel the cool breeze long before you reach the water.

Winds can be destructive, but most of the time we are happy to feel a gentle breeze. Part of the reason the equator is so warm is because of its lack of wind. The hot air around the middle of the earth moves straight up instead of going east or west. The middle band of the equator is called the doldrums. Sometimes we use this word to mean dull, listless, even despondent. There is little movement; everything sort of sits around.

Air movement is exactly what causes the famous monsoon season of Asia with its continual rain. As the land heats up, it makes a huge amount of air go up. When that air rises, it calls for a massive need for cool air. Wind comes from thousands of miles away to take the place of the hot air that has risen. As that air moves across oceans, it picks up moisture. Arriving at its destination, the newly cool and moist air dumps its rain on the ground. And it keeps dumping and keeps dumping. Some areas that received almost no rain one month could be drenched with 25 inches the next.

Areas which frequently have monsoon seasons suffer from terrible extremes of parching heat and soaking storms. They get plenty of rain but unfortunately sometimes they get it at the wrong time.

By setting the world in motion and by giving us changing temperatures, God has provided us with the gift of wind. In the right amount it gives us coolness at the beaches as well as rain and dryness in their season. Out of His treasure chest of marvelous works, God has given the wind as one of His greatest gifts.

"He makes mists rise throughout the earth and sends the lightning to bring down the rain; and sends the winds from his treasuries" (Ps. 135:7).

1. What creates a cool breeze at a beach?
2. Why is the air so hot at the equator?
3. What good comes from winds?

thirty-six

Avoid This Animal

Frankly I have not met one of these animals. And yet, I'm fairly sure I don't want to meet one. The thought of some animals sends chills up my back. High on my list of undesirable characters is the gruesome hyena.

If you dislike someone you haven't even met, it's called prejudice. I have a terrible prejudice against this ugly little creature. Consider some of the facts about hyenas for yourself.

Normally they spend their nights looking for dead bodies of other animals. If one can find a dead zebra or buffalo, it can spend a couple of weeks chewing on its body. It will eat the flesh, crack open the bones and then finish them off for dessert. When hyenas travel in a group, they may complete their meal much more quickly.

You aren't likely to meet a hyena unless you live in Africa or Asia. Some hyenas have spots on their bodies while others carry stripes. Probably their most famous trademark is their blood-curdling laugh. It's not really a laugh, and it's doubtful that this scavenger has much of a sense of humor.

Recently, it has been discovered that hyenas enjoy a wider diet than just carcasses. They appreciate four or five dozen crocodile eggs for breakfast if they get the chance. Hyenas have also been discovered to be hunters. They are willing to kill game, especially if it's weak or young and straying from its herd.

Gazelles, wildebeest and zebra can be found on their menu of living game. After the kill they may have to fight other animals in order to eat their prize. If a hyena does not complete its meal, there are plenty of birds, rats and other creatures around to finish it off.

Not restricted to fine dining, a hyena is willing to sink its teeth into a truck and bite into a generator. In some circumstances, a hyena will attack a human being.

Hyenas are good mothers who patiently feed and care for their cubs. Some will supply milk for their playful little offspring for almost a year and a half.

Granted, it isn't fair for me to dislike a hyena I have not even met. In my mind I know there are many other animals that eat carcasses. I also know that some of the ugliest animals are also some of the most cuddly and lovable.

But until I get to know hyenas a bit better, I think I'll keep my distance. Maybe someday a friend will convince me that hyenas have great personalities and I would find them fantastic pets. But until then . . . I think I'll stick with puppies and kittens.

The same thing is true of people. We need to stay away from strangers until we know more about them. They may turn out to be terrific but we can't be sure—not yet. Children need to be especially careful. The safest way to meet new adults is after your parents have met them first.

Sad to say, there are some evil people who want to hurt others. It pays to be careful.

"Avoid their haunts—turn away, go somewhere else, for evil men don't sleep until they've done their evil deed for the day. They can't rest unless they cause someone to stumble and fall" (Prov. 4:15, 16).

1. What do hyenas eat?
2. Are hyenas good mothers?
3. Why should you be careful about strangers?

thirty-seven

Do Spiders Have Ears?

Hannah, my friend in Colorado Springs, had an interesting question about spiders. She wanted to know if these busy little creatures have ears. If not, how do they hear?

The answer to the first question is easy. Spiders don't have ears. Question number two is the tough one. It may be that spiders can't hear at all. However, another possibility is that they hear vibrations or sound movements through the tiny hairs on their bodies. These hairs contain nerves and could send sound waves through the spider's system.

There are so many spiders in the world that we only see a small percentage of them. When we do see spiders, it looks like there is only one to a web or possibly two at the most. To look at a spider you might think it is so ugly that surely it couldn't have any friends. If you see a tree or part of a field with a large spider web, you may very well be looking at a colony of spiders rather than a loner.

A few spiders do like to work alone, but most of the 40,000 species of spiders would rather live in groups. They squeeze into tight spaces all over the world. Not only do they like to take over buildings, basements and attics, but they love the outdoors. If you walk into almost any field, you will be in the middle of thousands of spiders.

In some areas spiders prefer to cooperate in building one huge web. Often thousands of spiders will work together to construct a gigantic net. Frequently a large colony of spiders will consist of 5,000 to 8,000 members. In a few cases they have reached 100,000 in number.

Spiders are not as friendly as ants or bees, one big family working together. Rather, spiders make webs much as quilts are made. Each spider makes its own section of the web and then they tie them together. If any part of the web becomes broken, it is each spider's responsibility to repair only its own section.

When a victim gets caught in part of the web, the meal belongs to the builder of that part alone. If there is a misunderstanding over who owns the food or a boundary line, a terrible fight can break out between neighbor spiders.

A colony or community of spiders is found more often in areas where there is plenty of moisture and trees. These areas offer more food and consequently will support a greater number of spiders. In dry, barren regions fewer spiders live together.

Despite the difficulties of working together, the benefits are excellent. Because spiders manage to get along, they build a much larger web than they could do alone. A large web means food for each spider. It is easier for an insect to escape from a single web, but a group web is a much better trap. A bigger web is also more likely to capture insects of greater size.

Early in the morning, just before most of us awake, the colony of spiders finishes repairing their gigantic web. They have added touches to the net all night, and they scurry around to make sure it is finished.

As day breaks, members of the group sit back and take it easy. They are waiting for the rewards of their labor and when food arrives, they will be glad they managed to work together.

God made people so we, too, need to work together. Some individuals seem to get along alone but not most of us. We need each other. We help others when they are sad; we help each other celebrate when we are happy. If we stick close to each other, life goes better. Thank God for giving us relatives, friends and other Christians to help us when we need it.

"All the believers were together and had everything in common. Selling their possessions and goods, they gave to anyone as he had need" (Acts 2:44, 45 NIV).

1. Why do spiders build webs?
2. How do spiders work together?
3. How do we help each other?

thirty-eight

The Brave Pigeon

When you visit Washington, D.C., be sure to go to the Smithsonian Institution. Its buildings have so many things to see that you will want to spend several days there. Whatever else you have to miss, be sure to see Cher Ami. Cher Ami is a pigeon who has been there for many years. The pigeon is stuffed to serve as a reminder of genuine bravery by one of God's small creatures.

During World War I, communications were not as good as they are now. Consequently, if a message had to get through enemy lines, carrier pigeons were often used. It was dangerous work and naturally many pigeons were wounded and killed.

One battle in the war left a group of American soldiers trapped by the enemy. They tried to get messages out but with no success. Every carrier pigeon they sent was killed by the heavy fire.

Finally, the pigeon Cher Ami was chosen. The all-important note was tied to its leg and the pigeon was released to go for help. Extremely thick fire broke loose all around Cher Ami as it shot through the sky. Suddenly the pigeon was hit with a piece of metal smashing against its leg. Refusing to quit, Cher Ami pushed through the air and continued its long journey.

Almost half an hour later, courageous Cher Ami arrived at its destination. The pigeon's leg was torn and the note it carried barely hung on to its torn muscles.

We can't say how much Cher Ami knew about what it was doing, but we do know it stuck to the job. This famous pigeon knew it was supposed to travel from one point to another, and Cher Ami refused to allow even gunfire to stop it. That was a tremendous amount of courage whether Cher Ami knew it or not.

Courage is a rare and an important characteristic. It's hard to have enough courage to say no when you know you should, to turn something down just because you know it is wrong. But people do it even though it is tough.

It's also hard to say yes when you know you should. It's difficult to help out, to reach out, to share with others. You might be rejected, made fun of, even insulted.

A person has to have courage to follow the teaching of the Bible and of Jesus Christ. But people do it. And when they do, they feel great because they know it was right.

"Be ye therefore very courageous to keep and to do all that is written in the book of the Law of Moses" (Josh. 23:6, KJV).

1. Tell about Cher Ami.
2. Define courage.
3. Tell about some act of courage you have seen.

thirty-nine

Some Snakes Are Wimps

Most snakes are harmless creatures wiggling across the ground trying to pick up a meal. Usually they are happy to gulp down a mouse now and then, or maybe swallow a frog for dessert. If they need a bedtime snack, they might sample a couple of earthworms. Generally speaking, life is dull for them.

If a snake gets any excitement at all, it will probably come from a frightened mother with a garden hoe. If it lives in an open area, eagles might try to grab it. Lately, highways, construction sights and huge farm equipment have made its life pretty uncomfortable.

No child should touch a snake without checking with his parents first. What many of us see in our yards is the harmless garter, or garden snake. Many of these are colored basic olive, brown or black, complete with a racing stripe along their sides.

Garter snakes seldom get over three feet long. In most cases if a person finds a garter snake in the grass, a high speed race begins immediately. The person tears off in one direction and the snake shoots off in the other. Neither one wants anything to do with the other.

Some yards are the happy hunting grounds of the famous hognose snake. This snake is basically a wimp. It likes to pretend it is dangerous, but in reality it could barely hurt a human being at all.

If you surprise a hognose snake, it goes right into its mean act. The hognose will puff up its body and spread its neck to look like a cobra. It even makes a hissing noise in hopes of sending you into the house screaming.

But remember, the hognose snake is a wimp. If a person runs away, this snake crawls proudly away thinking it is pretty tough. However, if you yell at the hognose it will fold up like an old chair. It will roll over on its back and pretend to be dead. Now it hopes you will walk away and leave it alone. It's a wimp.

Temptation is much like the hognose snake. At first it looks tough. You think to yourself, "It would be all right to steal that" or "I had better lie and get out of this mess." It sounds good and we think we can't turn it down. Maybe we better do it.

Like the hognose, temptation looks tough at first. Maybe we should give in and do it.

But temptation is also a wimp. If we tell it to go away, it does. If we give in to temptation, it feels powerful.

The Bible tells us that we should tell temptation to take a hike. If we do, it will roll over and play dead, just like the hognose snake.

"So give yourselves humbly to God. Resist the devil and he will flee from you" (James 4:7).

1. What does a garter snake do if it sees a person?
2. What does a hognose snake do if it is frightened?
3. What should a person do when he meets temptation?

forty

Counting Fish Scales

If fish could talk to human beings, they would have unbelievable stories to tell. Fish have seen beautiful sights that we can only try to imagine. They could also tell horrible tales that we don't want to think about.

Their striking world has colorful creatures like the clown fish, which is decorated with a bright face similar to a circus clown. Some fish put on "pajamas" at night just before they go to sleep. Each evening these fish merely change colors and settle into matching rocks. All night long they rest safely in their "pajamas" while their enemies swim by looking for them.

Some fish have been living under water for a long time. With many it is nearly impossible to tell how old they really are. Without gray hair or receding hairlines, it is hard to even guess. However, if a fish has scales, that is one way to estimate its age.

Much like the rings in a tree trunk, a fish's scales grow as it grows. Each year they extend a little farther. Counting the number of times they have stretched out helps determine its age. Often it takes a capable biologist to do this.

We can do this with a dead fish but don't try to examine the scales on a pet. Fish have a liquid like oil covering their scales. If we rub that oil off, the fish loses a protection it must have. It would also be unwise to push, pull or squish its scales since they need to be in order.

When you do examine a set of scales, notice the way they overlap each other in neat fashion. Like feathers or roof tiles, they are tightly fitted to keep practically everything out. Many fish do not have scales and some varieties have only part of their bodies covered with scales. A few mammals like the pangolin anteater have scales also.

If properly cared for, some fish live many years. Though few live this long, some goldfish could possibly live to celebrate their 25th birthday. The biggest obstacle to reaching old age is other creatures that want to eat them. When cared for properly, a catfish could live for 60 years.

Every once in a while fish must see some unforgettable sights. They have seen diamond rings sink aimlessly to the bottom. Some have watched gigantic ships sink past them. Others have looked at men and women as they swam by in scuba outfits.

They have seen a great deal that we have not seen. And if they could talk, they could tell you that God has been good. Job told us that even a fish could tell you that God has given us all we need.

Nature is a living testimony that God is real. The next time you see a fish, say to yourself, "That fish has seen some of God's ability that I will never see." Even the fish knows that God is good.

"Who doesn't know that the Lord does things like that? Ask the dumbest beast—he knows that it is so; ask the birds—they will tell you; or let the earth teach you, or the fish of the sea" (Job 12:7, 8, 9).

1. How can a biologist determine the age of a fish?
2. What is the biggest obstacle to a fish reaching old age?
3. How does nature show that God is good?

forty-one

When the Sting Is Gone

"I'm sorry we have kept you waiting," said the voice on the phone. "Lisa was stung by a bee, and I had to take her directly to the hospital."

Some people are allergic to bee stings and can become very sick. A small number of people die from such stings. Those who have had bad reactions often carry medicine in their car or in their purse in case they get stung.

For most of us a bee sting is painful, but the pain will soon go away. Once we are stung we are very careful to keep a good distance from bees or anything else that can sting.

If a honeybee should sting you, you don't have to worry about the bee anymore. The action of stinging you actually killed it. However, you might still want to keep an eye on its relatives.

When a doctor gives you a shot with a needle or a hypodermic syringe he or she is doing the same thing a bee would. The bee makes a small hole in your skin. The bee then pushes its poison into your body. That's enough to cause you plenty of pain and often a good deal of swelling.

As if bees were not enough to be concerned about, there are other creatures that could sting you just as well. One of them is the hornet or wasp. You have seen them flying around houses or barns. They often build their homes high up in doorways or in attics.

The bad thing about a hornet or wasp is that they do not die when they sting. They could be on the prowl for you a second time. It might be better if your parents could remove the hornet nest from near your house.

If you live in certain warm climates, you have an extra creature to watch out for. It is called a scorpion and it carries a nasty sting in its tail. Most scorpions are only a couple of inches long but can give you a lot of pain.

There are 500 different species of scorpions in the world and 12 of those live in Israel. They were there both during the time of Moses and the time of Jesus Christ.

Normally scorpions avoid people. However, if attacked or surprised, they defend themselves very quickly. Their sting will hurt but they do not carry enough poison to kill a person in good health.

Avoiding the heat of the day, many scorpions prefer to hide and go hunting during the early evening. Scorpions have a pair of sharp, crab-like pinchers which they use to hold their prey while they zap them with the stinger in their tail.

Maybe Paul had the scorpion in mind when he wrote about death. He told us the Christian no longer has to fear the sting of death. It is still there but the pain is gone. Death has lost its sting. A scorpion without a stinger would still be there, but we would have little to fear.

Jesus Christ has made sure that death cannot hurt the believer.

"O death, where then your victory? Where then your sting? For sin—the sting that causes death—will all be gone; and the law, which reveals our sins, will no longer be our judge" (1 Cor. 15:55, 56).

1. Can a honeybee sting you twice?
2. Where do hornets build nests?
3. What does Paul say about the sting of death?

forty-two

Not Looking for Trouble

If a hedgehog had its way, it would live every day in quiet and peace. A low-key figure, a hedgehog doesn't even like to work in unpleasant weather. If the animal gets too hot, it gives up most activities; and if it should turn cold, the hedgehog will take the first opportunity to hibernate.

But don't let this relaxed creature fool you. If anything wants to do battle, the hedgehog will turn immediately into a mean, fighting machine. It is equipped with sharp teeth and quills like a porcupine. A hedgehog moves slowly but is not afraid to swim a stream or climb a tree. In fact, it isn't afraid to do many things since it has tough skin and can roll into a ball that makes it practically impossible to hurt.

Like porcupines, hedgehogs cannot throw their quills, but they are painful weapons. Every once in a while they like to shine them up, possibly just to frighten enemies. A hedgehog will begin by licking smooth objects, like rocks, until its mouth is watering with saliva. It will then reach around and lick each of its sharp quills. Maybe they are merely trying to stay clean, or possibly they are showing off their swords.

Occasionally a hedgehog will be attacked by a snake. However, this animal doesn't get too excited about the creeping creature. Often a hedgehog will tease and let the snake try to get it, which might look like easy work to the attacker, but the snake soon learns the hedgehog is very tough. The hedgehog plays his own form of tag until finally the snake lies down exhausted. At that point the hedgehog goes over and makes

short work of the snake. A snake may have high hopes of what it will do, but it will probably end up as dinner.

Many of us have never seen a hedgehog. These creatures live mostly in China, Europe, Britain, Africa and Asia Minor.

Animals are much like people. Some creatures are ill-tempered and get angry at practically anything. They look for fights and seem willing to take on animals of any size. Without looking for food they appear to enjoy causing pain and starting arguments.

Other animals are content with a calm nature. The hedgehog is one of those; it is a lover of peace.

We don't prove we're strong by starting fights. People who have to quarrel half the time must be pretty miserable characters.

Jesus believed that those who work for peace are wiser than those who try to start fights. Living at peace is much closer to how God intended for people to live.

"Happy are those who strive for peace—they shall be called the sons of God" (Matt. 5:9).

1. How does a hedgehog spend the winter?
2. How does a hedgehog defend itself?
3. Do you know someone who is a lover of peace? Explain.

forty-three

The Mantis Parent

Nature has many good parents. Some animals care for their young and will fight to keep them safe. The praying mantis is an interesting insect which usually leaves its newborn alone to face whatever trouble there is in life. A large part of nature ignores its young, and the results are frequently disastrous.

The praying mantis received its name because it looks like it could be praying. Its hands are folded at its face and its head is slightly bowed. However, looks can fool us. Actually the mantis can be extremely tough and in its own world is feared by many creatures.

One of the reasons why many people like the praying mantis is that it has a large appetite. It loves to eat insects. Some farmers like to have them around just to cut down on the number of insects in their fields.

The praying mantis menu does not call for dead or cooked insects, either. They enjoy their meals fresh and alive. The mantis is patient for a good dinner and will merely wait in the leaves until a tasty morsel comes by. Not a picky eater, it will be happy with a Japanese beetle, a bee, a moth, a grasshopper, or a wasp or practically any bug-like creature.

When its victim comes close, the mantis strikes like a bullet and jumps on the insect's back. Holding it firmly in its strong forelegs, the praying mantis takes a few well-aimed bites out of its prey and the rest is strictly mealtime.

The praying mantis has to be careful, however. It has a few of its own enemies sneaking around. Skunks, birds and monkeys like to fill out their diet with a couple of choice mantises.

Most of us have seen a praying mantis, but there is much more to the story than we might think. There are 1,800 different varieties of mantises and they live in most of the world. They come in a large assortment of colors, everything from green to gray to brown to brilliant pink.

It all sounds like gruesome business, insects attacking and eating each other, but that is the natural cycle. If the praying mantis, bird, reptile and others did not eat insects, we would soon be overrun with bugs destroying our crops, plants and trees. God has apparently sent them here to hold the lower creatures in check.

The praying mantis may be good at many things, but it appears that as a parent it gets especially poor grades. They are excellent at reproducing, but seem to lack basic parental skills. A praying mantis probably makes no attempt to protect its eggs. After the eggs are hatched, the tiny insects are left to struggle for themselves. The result is confusion for the newborn which can be easily eaten. Not only that, but the young frequently eat each other also.

It comes as no surprise that the mantis family is not close. In most cases the female mantis ate father mantis long before the eggs hatched.

Children who have good parents have a great deal to thank God for. That's exactly what God wanted us to have—parents who are caring, patient, kind and loving.

When you grow up, you may have the chance to be just that type of parent. God had a terrific idea when He created good parents. They watch carefully over their children.

"Rather, bring them up with the loving discipline the Lord himself approves, with suggestions and godly advice" (Eph. 6:4).

1. Where did the name praying mantis come from?
2. Why do farmers like praying mantises?
3. What kind of parent do you want to be?

forty-four

Building Stone Houses

All of us know of animals that build their own homes. Some collect twigs to make nests and add a bit of straw to give comfort. There are wasps that construct homes of mud or clay. One of the most unusual homebuilders is the caddis, which builds an underwater home out of pebbles and glues them together for strength.

A mother caddis will lay hundreds of eggs in the water. She looks much like a butterfly but usually lacks the bright colors. There are 3,000 different types of caddis. The caddis spends most of its life as a youngster. It is in the larva stage for an entire year, but may live less than a month as an adult.

Not every caddis larva builds a strong home. Some are content with nests. But if you build a home in a mountain stream, you had better make sure the stones will stick together. This is where the caddis' special glue kit comes in handy. An unusual cement-like paste comes out of its head, and the caddis applies this to the stones. The glue is water-resistant and strong enough to hold under water.

When the young caddis starts to construct its home, it begins by looking for bright-colored pebbles. Red, white and black stones are gathered for the project and other shiny objects might be added.

A baby caddis would be an easy victim for any fish that wandered along if it did not find good protection. In fact, the biggest purpose a caddis has may be to feed fish. While many creatures would simply hide in any place that is open, the caddis would rather have a stable home that is built correctly and offers the most protection.

You might see a caddis if you visit the mountains, but you have to know what to look for. As adults they leave the water and fly. They look a great deal like moths.

How does a baby or larva caddis know how to build a stone house and glue it together? Somehow God placed an instinct in the caddis that allows it to drive toward that goal. And since it already has the glue in its head, this becomes the natural urge to follow.

If a caddis is to depend on its stone house, the cement or glue has to hold. It must be adhesive and yet water-resistant at the same time. If it did not hold, the house could crumble and fish would eat the caddis.

When some things do not hold, the result is often disaster. The Bible tells us to hold on to the good and godly things in life. If we let go and start reaching for things that are evil, our lives will soon start to crumble.

Christ helps us to hold on. He is like the glue. By following Him we can hold on to what is good.

"Test everything. Hold on to the good" (1 Thess. 5:21 NIV).

1. Where does the caddis carry its glue supply?
2. Describe the caddis' home.
3. What good things can you hold on to?

forty-five

The Young Deer

There aren't many animals as cute as the white-tailed baby deer. Called fawns, they are usually born in the spring and stay close to their mother for almost a year. The fawn's spots help it hide while it is young. By September the spots begin to disappear and the deer takes on an adult appearance.

If you have ever seen a deer standing in a field, you know how captivating they look. In the midwest we occasionally see a deer bounding among the trees. Sometimes they will stand on a dirt road and stare as your car approaches. Today I saw the small hoof marks of a deer on a muddy road in Nebraska.

The correct terms for deer are the fawn, the doe and the buck. A fawn is a baby deer like Bambi. A doe is a female adult or a mother deer. A buck is an adult male or a father.

A buck or father deer grows an impressive looking set of antlers. Every year its antlers fall off and it grows a new set. With so many antlers being dropped every year, why aren't there plenty to be found in the woods? The main reason is that nature provides many creatures to tidy up. A number of animals, including rabbits and mice, enjoy munching on tough antlers. If you're lucky enough to find a set, you know the animals have not had time to finish them off.

When a fawn is born it has a close relationship with its mother. At first an awkward youngster, the fawn soon develops strong enough legs to wander around by itself. The mother keeps a close eye on the new offspring. If a fawn roams too far or gets too close to danger, the doe is quick to call its child back. The mother will really scold the fawn so it will not do it again. Sometimes the mother deer will give the fawn a sharp smack with its head, nothing long or abusive, just enough to get the fawn's attention.

We can't begin to calculate how many young deer have been rescued because they have a caring mother. Sometimes fawns need to be stopped simply for their own good.

Their need for good discipline from their parents is much the same as we need. There are many troubles and dangers that could hurt children if they had no parents to warn them.

Once in a while words may not be enough. A quick rap on the back side, maybe a firm tap on the hand, will be plenty of warning to a child. Some parents would rather sit a child in a corner and take the T.V. away. However, a smack on the rear might save many children from serious harm.

"Sometimes mere words are not enough—discipline is needed. For the words may not be heeded" (Prov. 29:19).

1. What is a fawn? A doe? A buck?
2. Why don't we find many deer antlers in the woods?
3. If you were a parent, how would you discipline your child?

forty-six

Stuck Up a Tree

Maybe you're one of the millions of Americans who love cats. People enjoy cats of all sizes, colors and personalities. They keep cats as friends, playmates for their children, and to catch mice around their house and yard.

Any cat lover can tell you what an excellent animal a cat can be. They can sit in your lap while you read, follow you from room to room to keep you company, and they are energetic wrestlers. A piece of string or a ball is all you need for entertainment.

When a child first gets a kitten, he needs some simple instructions on how to treat it. We had one friend who came home after work, opened the refrigerator door and his cat jumped out. After that he had a long talk with his son. Another family heard some thumping in their clothes dryer. They arrived just in time to rescue their kittens.

Most of the time children and kittens mix well. Kittens provide an outstanding opportunity to teach responsibility and mutual caring.

After a young person has gotten to know a kitten well, he can understand the language of a cat. Kittens like to purr. Most of the time it means they are happy or content. It also means the child is doing a good job of feeding, watering and caring for his pet. A child also learns what noises the kitten makes if it is hungry or doesn't feel well.

One of the activities a kitten enjoys most is to have its fur stroked and rubbed. A gentle touch tells the kitten that you care and everything is fine. Stroking a kitten is also good for people. Touching tends to calm us down and make us feel at peace.

Cats are fortunate if they can be raised by their mothers. They have some of the most considerate mothers in nature. Not only do mother cats feed their kittens, but they also keep them clean. Using her tongue for a washcloth, mother sees to it that her kittens are dirt-free from head to tail.

A mother cat will also teach her kittens. They will learn to stalk birds or mice. She will show them how to stretch their bodies out as they tiptoe under a tree. Mother will also teach them the difficult art of backing down a tree. Not a skill easily mastered, it is one that most cats will need. If the cat fails to learn this, some poor pet owner will have to haul out his ladder and rescue his timid friend.

Kittens that have mothers to help them grow up are fortunate. Children who have mothers may be even more fortunate. Mothers can be loving, listening and helpful. They can teach us to care for our things, to bake, and to brush our teeth. Mothers can remind us of things we forget, like books, jackets and saying thank you. And when you need it the most, they are terrific at giving hugs.

If you have a good mother, maybe you will want to tell her so. And don't forget to thank God for her, too.

"Her children stand and bless her; so does her husband" (Prov. 31:28).

1. Name three things a mother cat teaches her kittens.
2. What animal do you think is the best pet?
3. What do you like most about mothers?

forty-seven

Who Loves Mosquitoes?

When a mosquito lands on your arm, you know exactly why it's there. The puny pest is going to run its tube into your flesh. And you know why it's doing that? It wants to draw out your blood. If its eggs are to develop, they must have blood. It would prefer animal blood, but it will settle for yours.

The tube that pierced your flesh is no simple instrument. Part of it does the cutting. Part draws out blood. And another part merely pours in mosquito saliva. The saliva keeps your blood from clogging in his tube.

Mosquito saliva is something your body doesn't want. Saliva causes the swelling and itching that most of us experience. People are different and some will hardly swell at all. Others react to the saliva with large bumps on their skin.

It is the saliva that carries a number of sicknesses that can be deadly to human beings. Yellow fever, malaria and encephalitis are a few of the killer diseases mosquitoes carry.

The world is not in immediate danger of running out of mosquitoes. One female can lay 400 eggs at one time. They can do that several times in one summer. Nor are we about to run out of variety. There are over 2,000 different species of mosquitos. My personal favorites would be the ones that do not hunt for blood.

Mosquitoes are excellent fliers. They have all the ability of a helicopter plus. They can hover over an area, go up and down or take off in a flash. In a struggle they become outstanding fighter pilots. Darting in and out, they are tough for humans to catch in flight.

Fortunately, birds, frogs and fish have less trouble catching mosquitoes. They feed on them regularly. One-third of all mosquitoes are eaten within one day of hatching. However, their rate of reproducing is so high that their numbers remain large.

These little pests seem to be drawn to man because they like our breath. The feel of warm, moist carbon dioxide convinces the mosquito that you must have a good supply of luscious blood in you.

Despite all the problems mosquitoes represent, there is good news. Formerly many people and animals died from the diseases carried by these insects. Today medicine has been able to control these diseases. We can thank God that many of us are safe. There are areas in the world where mosquitoes still cause illness and death. Maybe we can help missionaries and doctors deliver the medicines necessary to wipe out these horrible sicknesses.

We are thankful that most of us are free from mosquito-related diseases. It is very sad that some of us are not free yet.

"Always give thanks for everything to our God and Father in the name of our Lord Jesus Christ" (Eph. 5:20).

1. What causes swelling from a mosquito bite?
2. What animals feed on mosquitos?
3. Why are mosquitoes drawn to man?

The Wirey Weasel

Where we live no one likes to be called a weasel. This cousin to the skunk has a bad reputation for sneaking around and, in many areas, for wiggling into chicken coops. They kill chickens, frequently destroying more than they really need for food.

Because of their long flexible bodies, weasels are hard to

keep out. Twisting their thin frames, they can squeeze through openings only a few inches wide.

In the wild, weasels play an important role in keeping other animal populations from growing too large. They love to eat mice, snakes, and frogs. Even a few meals of rabbit or squirrel come in handy. Weasels are willing to munch on earthworms or attack a potential dinner much larger than themselves.

An aggressive hunter, the weasel will chase mice between rocks and race through hollow logs. If they have to, they will push their wirey bodies into the homes of mice, looking for food.

After emptying a mouse house, the weasel may choose to convert it into a den for its family. Most weasels like to decorate their den in soft, warm colors. They line the interior with feathers and fur previously worn by their victims.

Weasels are difficult to see during the winter because of the subways they build through the snow. Preferring to travel at night, they can move great distances through these tunnels without fear of being caught by human beings. They also need not fear their toughest enemy, the great horned owl. If caught in the open, the weasel is picked off by the owl.

The weasels which live in snowy climates experience a change in the color of their fur. Called ermine, this white winter fur is considered valuable to man.

Most of the time weasels go quietly about their job keeping a balance in nature. Once in a great while they shoot off a musk which smells much like their relative, the skunk. They are not large animals, only measuring 6 to 18 inches long at the most.

People would probably have a fairly high opinion of them if it were not for their nasty habit of stealing chickens. Chicken theft has given them a bad name. It's a hard reputation to get rid of. Bad names stick. Often for hundreds of years.

People seem to have the same trouble with names. Once you get a bad reputation, it's really hard to get rid of. A thief or a liar or a gossip or a cheat is a title that's difficult to shake. The person may stop stealing and become an excellent individual. He may become a Christian and change entirely. Nevertheless the name might hang on.

It's far better to keep your name clean in the first place.

"If you must choose, take a good name rather than great riches; for to be held in loving esteem is better than silver and gold" (Prov. 22:1).

1. Why are weasels hard to keep out of chicken coops?
2. What else besides chickens do they eat?
3. How do you get a good reputation?

forty-nine

Can Quicksand Swallow You?

Few parts of nature sound as terrible as the thought of quicksand. We often picture a person walking out onto a sandy area and suddenly being pulled beneath the sand.

Before we let our imagination run away with us, we should look at this a bit closer. First, consider a couple of facts. There are areas of quicksand in the world and people have died in quicksand. Animals have also perished there.

However, quicksand is not exactly what many of us believe. Some seacoasts, streams and rivers have soft spots we call quicksand. These areas are a mixture of sand and water. Their surface *looks* firm and a casual walker or wader may think it will support his weight. Yet when a person steps on that spot the sand gives way and the person will start to sink. As he sinks, sand will rise to the top as if he were being pulled under.

It's much like stepping into a water hole. The person, however, is surprised because he thought the sand would hold him. Instantly the sand gives way, but it is not capable of sucking a person under.

To survive, the victim needs simply to lie on his back. He will float on the watery sand much as he would on water. Most of those who die in quicksand probably did not know they could have floated.

Books and movies have given horrible descriptions of the mysterious power of quicksand. Those who are familiar with the facts have little to fear.

Today construction goes on in quicksand. Builders use specially designed foundations to hold their structures. Others add chemicals to help change the thickness of the sand.

There are dangers in the rivers and seas we visit. However, there are not as many as we hear about. The more we learn about nature the more safely we can enjoy it. Old myths and exaggerations aren't much help to anyone.

The same principle is true about God. Many things are said about Him that are not true. When we learn what God is really like, it is easier to love Him and feel His love for us.

Understanding Jesus Christ is a big step to knowing the truth about God.

"And you will know the truth, and the truth will set you free" *(John 8:32).*

1. How can a person survive if he is in quicksand?
2. How are buildings constructed in quicksand?
3. What are some ways to learn more facts about God?

fifty

The Intelligent Raven

What do you think of when you hear the word "raven"? Do you picture a thief stealing crops? Do you imagine a blackbird so smart it can talk? Maybe you think of a scout leading people to find food.

All of these ideas about ravens plus a good many more are true. The raven can live in the bitter cold of the Arctic or in the heat of southern Mexico. They can build nests in the Sahara Desert or live comfortably in the Himalayan Mountains.

Ravens make good pets for those who are willing to study birds. They can be taught to say words, and some owners insist they know what they are saying. A raven can also be trained to perform tricks; however, don't be surprised if it steals your rings. They have a terrible reputation for "borrowing" things that do not belong to them.

If you have something a raven really wants, it may find another raven to help fool you. One raven will get your attention by doing tricks for you. While you watch its antics in amazement, the second raven will quietly sneak up behind you and steal the object it wants.

Ravens have also been known to make deals. If you have food it wants, the raven might bring you an object in exchange. It could deliver a stone or a stick. If you decide to deal with the raven, it might bring you a second one.

Are ravens smart enough to lead people to find food? That's a hard one to answer. Some hunters insist it's true. They will follow ravens and as a result find a herd of animals. What really happened? Did the ravens accidentally pass over hunters on their way to a herd? Or did they want people to see them fly over? Possibly they wanted the people to follow and hunt the animals. The ravens would then be able to feed on the remains.

Some hunters believe the ravens led them. Therefore, they leave some meat as a reward for the blackbirds.

It will surprise some to learn that the ravens are good parents and family members. A raven mates with one bird for life. The relationship can last for 15 years or more.

They are also excellent parents to a nest of very demanding youngsters. Since the young are constantly crying for food, the parents must make as many as 45 trips daily from their nest in search of food.

Despite this constant need for food, ravens do not seem to go hungry. The number of ravens in the world remains high as God has provided them with good sense and plenty of food.

It's hard to picture a raven perched on a telephone pole worrying about its next meal. Jesus had trouble imagining worry lines on a bird's forehead. He told us the raven doesn't have half the ability we have and yet it doesn't fret about surviving. God takes care of the raven's needs. He is also willing to meet the needs of people who trust Him.

"Look at the ravens—they don't plant or harvest or have barns to store away their food, and yet they get along all right—for God feeds them. And you are far more valuable to him than any birds!" (Luke 12:24).

1. How do two ravens work together to fool a person?
2. Are ravens good parents?
3. How did Jesus use the ravens to teach His followers?

fifty-one

Black Widow Spiders at Work

Do you ever feel useless? Do you have days when you feel as if you can't do anything right? That is the way most of us feel sometimes. Fortunately you are really one of the most useful of all of God's creations. There are so many things you can do and enjoy.

If you want to talk about something useless, imagine the middle strand in one thread of a spider's web. What good could anything that tiny possibly be? Well, science has found an important use for this almost invisible piece of material.

When companies build surveying instruments, they need a thin thread to use for the crosshair. A crosshair marks the middle of their lens.

You might think any piece of thread would serve for this job, but that's not correct. A human hair is 80 times thicker than a thread from a spider web.

The exact spider web the company is looking for belongs to the black widow spider. Their web strands are so thin that most people have trouble seeing them. That works perfect for the surveyor's instrument since the thread is magnified 30 times its actual size. Despite its thinness the thread is tough and will not break easily.

Even a spider web is thicker than the company really wants. When they find a web, they must carefully pull the thread apart. It is the tiny center part they are really looking for.

Since a black widow spider is extremely poisonous, the worker has to handle it carefully. If the spider doesn't feel like spinning a web, the worker gets one of the strangest jobs in the world. He has to gently and carefully rub the belly of the spider. Soon the happy little spider begins spinning out its web.

If we have learned to use a black widow spider web—no, make that the middle strand of a black widow spider web— think how valuable a human being like you must be.

You are never useless, even if you sometimes feel that way. There are too many things you can do. There are too many people you can help. There are too many ways you can serve God.

And you are more valuable than many, many middle strands from a black widow spider's web.

"Serve the Lord with gladness" (Ps. 100:2, KJV).

1. How is the middle strand of a black widow spider's web used in industry?
2. Why was it chosen?
3. Name five ways you are useful to others.

fifty-two

Chimps Are Comedians

Have you watched chimpanzees running around in a zoo? Maybe you have seen them in an outdoor show. They can rollerskate, ride motorcycles and wear strange clothing. Do chimps realize that they are being funny or are they doing it by accident?

Those who have studied chimpanzees for years have decided that chimps know exactly what they are doing. They enjoy being ridiculous; they like to make people laugh.

Even chimps that do not live around people like to play clown for themselves and other chimpanzees. They don't have to be taught to act funny. As tiny babies they begin making faces and playing games. Mother chimps play peekaboo with their babies and send them into long giggling attacks.

As they grow older, chimps like to tease each other. They try to make other chimpanzees laugh and often collapse in laughter while they are trying.

Given a pile of hats, chimps will often try them on in order to make people laugh. By no means a sad faced comedian, they get caught up in the action and laugh as loudly as anyone. Chimps have expressive faces and use them to communicate a wide range of emotions.

Chimpanzees are considered one of the most intelligent animals. They are fairly easy to train and seem to learn a wide range of human activities. They can be taught to dress themselves and brush their teeth. One chimp was able to master the game of tic-tac-toe and make its own decisions.

Other great apes might be as intelligent as the chimpanzee, but it is hard to know. The orangutan is shy and less willing to show off. Therefore it doesn't seem as quick or as sharp as its chimp relatives. Yet, more tests may show it to have great mental abilities.

There are several reasons to keep a safe distance from chimpanzees. For one thing, they can have bad tempers and are much stronger than humans. Another reason is their surprising humor. At any moment a chimp might gulp a mouthful of water and then playfully spit it all over the people watching. It will then laugh loudly and long at the soaked victims.

Laughter is an important part of a healthy, happy life. Maybe that's why God created it. When it doesn't hurt anyone, laughter makes people feel good about themselves and about others. Possibly God watches us and laughs every once in a while.

"A time to laugh" (Eccles. 3:4).

1. Name one thing a chimp can be taught to do.
2. Besides the chimp, name another member of the ape family.
3. Tell a situation where you and your family have laughed together.